ORGANIZING CLASSROOMS FOR SMALL-GROUP INSTRUCTION

LEARNING FOR MASTERY

Carolyn M. Lawrence
Gordon Lawrence
Linda S. Samek

D1604139

Rowman & Littlefield Education
Lanham, Maryland • Toronto • Oxford
2006

Published in the United States of America
by Rowman & Littlefield Education
A Division of Rowman & Littlefield Publishers, Inc.
A wholly owned subsidiary of
The Rowman & Littlefield Publishing Group, Inc.
4501 Forbes Boulevard, Suite 200, Lanham, Maryland 20706
www.rowmaneducation.com

PO Box 317
Oxford
OX2 9RU, UK

British Library Cataloguing in Publication Information Available

Library of Congress Cataloging-in-Publication Data

Lawrence, Carolyn M.
  Organizing classrooms for small-group instruction : learning for mastery /
Carolyn M. Lawrence, Gordon Lawrence, Linda Samek.
    p. cm.
  ISBN-13: 978-1-57886-356-3 (hardcover : alk. paper)
  ISBN-10: 1-57886-356-2 (hardcover : alk. paper)
  ISBN-13: 978-1-57886-357-0 (pbk. : alk. paper)
  ISBN-10: 1-57886-357-0 (pbk. : alk. paper)
  1. Mastery learning. 2. Group work in education. I. Lawrence, Gordon,
1930– II. Samek, Linda S. III. Title.

  LB1031.4.L39 2006
  372.139'5—dc22
                                                    2005031178

∞™ The paper used in this publication meets the minimum
requirements of American National Standard for Information
Sciences—Permanence of Paper for Printed Library Materials,
ANSI/NISO Z39.48-1992.
Manufactured in the United States of America.

CONTENTS

CONTENTS

1

A CENTERS APPROACH TO SMALL-GROUP INSTRUCTION

Five realities of elementary classrooms are very clear:

- Children come in a very wide range of achievement levels.
- Children's progress in the fundamentals of reading, writing, and mathematics depends largely on how well the teacher matches instruction to each child's level.
- When a teacher needs to connect with a child at his or her level, the teacher has to have a system—such as pulling small groups for reading or math—to allow one-to-one dialogue and observation.
- When a teacher works with a small group, the rest of the class has to be on its own—doing something such as seatwork.
- Research in classrooms has shown, without a doubt, that typical paper and pencil seatwork is by far the least efficient and effective component of instruction.

There's the dilemma. When the teacher's direct attention needs to be pulled from the whole group to a small group, the children who are working on their own do not use their time very well. This book is about a program of structured independent activities that engage students while the teacher works closely with a small group, such as a guided reading group. Designed to help teachers provide for the many achievement levels of children in any classroom, the program is essentially a system of centers for managing children's individual practice of skills. All the students are in the centers except the small group the teacher has scheduled to be with her for close instruction.

This chapter invites you to visit some centers in action, so you can see what we mean by structured, self-managing activities. Come along in your imagination. As you enter a classroom during the time that centers are in use, you see a few children sitting with the teacher while the others are actively involved in small groups or working alone. Some are sitting around tables or at

desks grouped together, some on the floor, some moving about quietly, some talking quietly to themselves or to a tablemate. Each center is devoted to some kind of common activity, designated by a bright cardboard sign hanging above it. You count six centers, in addition to the group of seven students working together with the teacher at a table.

The children who are not sitting with the teacher appear busy and focused on their work. As you glance at what they're doing, it's clear they are all practicing skills—but different skills at different achievement levels. Some are using paper and pencil, but most are working with a variety of manipulative materials with immediate, self-correcting feedback.

You spend the first few minutes in a center where four children are working with kits called *Stepboards* (listed in chapter 7). The Stepboard kits consist of plastic boards with indentations, 26 of which hold all the letters in alphabetical order. Each child has a set of 24 plastic strips color coded for the skill represented in the set. The strips present the same skill 24 times, beginning with an easy variation of the skill and progressing to a harder version of the same skill. Each set of strips contain practice of 24 strips, which the teacher has observed a particular child needs. Below the bank of letters is a slot for putting the strips, one at a time. Each strip contains a skill practice that calls for selecting letters to fit at the top edge of the strip. Because the strip has grooves at the top like a puzzle piece, the letters will only fit into the strip if the children pick the correct ones.

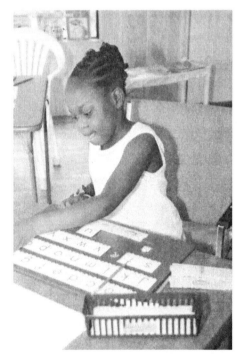

Center time has just started, and you hear Tom say to the rest of the group at this center, "Here's your record card. Pick up the box of strips that match the color written on your record card. Don't forget to mark the card when you finish each strip." (You later learn that Tom is the student assigned as captain of the center for this time slot.) Billy says, "I like to work these puzzles because we don't have to write the answers down." Tom says, "Yeah, but you got to mark your record card when you finish a strip." Tom and Joan are working on short vowel sounds while Billy and Joe are working on comprehension skills. The boards are identical, but each student has a different colored set of strips. You notice that this manipulative kit won't let any letter be inserted except the right one, and the children are using this self-correcting feature a lot, apparently without any embarrassment. They all like the instant feedback.

As you move on to the other centers, you find each one has its own set of directions along with the materials. A manila folder in each center contains each child's assignment for that center and a way to chart his or her progress throughout the assignment.

The next center you visit has as its centerpiece a 3-foot-by-2-foot U.S. map jigsaw puzzle. This appears to be a cooperative learning center. A closer look tells you the subject of the center is the 2004 election campaign.

The children work collectively to put the state-shaped pieces into the puzzle and identify the capitals of the states. The group's record card shows that the children have collectively completed this same center for four center times before today. All of the state pieces are in place. You can easily tell that the center gives the children practice in recognizing the relative size, shape, and location of the states and the names of their capitals (third graders). Following today's directions in the center, the children are attaching little flags made of toothpicks and small strips of paper. The strips have on them the state's name and the number of electoral votes allotted by its population size. One student tells you that when the election is over, they will make new flags out of red and blue paper to show which state went for which candidate, and they will add the electoral votes to show who won 270 votes. The teacher later tells you that he or she uses this center as a hands-on activity dealing with current events. At the end of each current events unit, students write a summary of what they learned.

Another center contains manipulative kits. The students sitting next to each other are using apparently identical tile-sets but have different level books to work with the tile boxes. As Angela and Darin sit side by side, they ask each other a question about what a picture may be or how to read a word. Although the levels of the books are not the same, there is no apparent stigma. These skills book/kits are called Versa-Tiles (see chapter 7). They consist of flat plastic boxes with a hinged bottom and lid that both have 12 indentations in them. The indentations in the base are marked by the letters *A* through *L*. The kit includes 12 tiles numbered 1 through 12 on one side and simple color-shapes on the bottom of each one. Darin finishes a page of 12 problems, having placed the 12 tiles in his box in a particular order, on top of the letters. He closes the box top, turns the box over, and opens it from the bottom. He smiles as he sees a geometric pattern formed by the 12 color shapes, showing that he has put the tiles in the correct order. The pattern matches the one on the page he has been using. He shows his pattern to Angela. Angela finishes her page, opens her box from the bottom, and sees a pattern that is right except for three pieces. She takes them out, closes the box and turns it over. Checking her assigned page, she sees how she got the tiles out of order. She rereads the questions in her booklet and puts the three tiles back in. This time the pattern is an exact match. Both children mark their record cards. These materials, too, provide feedback for self-correction.

As you walk around the room, you can easily see that all the centers contain materials on different skill levels. And while children in a center are doing similar work, it is obvious to you—but perhaps not to them—that they are working on different instructional levels. It appears that the teacher has identified where each child is in a skill sequence and has written the students' center assignments to put them at the right place in the sequenced materials.

In another center, marked by the letters *A* and *D*, children appear to be doing individual work that looks like a homework assignment. You later learn that this is a skills center with individual assignments that the teacher wishes to grade to see if the child has acquired skills previously taught. This center, the only one each child uses every day, is the one that requires the teacher to provide feedback by checking the children's responses—in the same way seatwork or homework would be checked.

You notice that the centers contain mostly familiar resources, ones that most teachers already have for teaching reading, writing, listening, specific language arts skills, math, and other skills. In one center you see students checking their work by using copies of the teacher's editions for the work assigned. Obviously, the children have been trained to work with the materials independently, without the teacher's assistance. They find the feedback they need in the materials and record their own work completions.

After you have been in the room about 20 minutes, the teacher rings a small bell. The children start gathering up and putting away their materials. They do it quietly, in a routine and orderly way. They mark their progress charts, put them in the folder, stand up, and push their chairs up to the table. The center captain checks that everything is in place. In exactly a minute, the bell rings again, and the children glance at a chart showing which center they are scheduled to go to next. Then they all move to new centers, except for eight children who go to the semicircular table at the teacher's desk. If you stayed in this classroom through the whole day, you'd find that there are four 20- to 25-minute rotations altogether. Each child visits three centers in addition to the guided reading time with the teacher. On the following day, he or she visits the other three centers. Center time lasts approximately 60 to 90 minutes per day or less.

If the teacher gave you an explanation of the centers program, it most likely would highlight the central feature of the program: all the centers provide for practice of skills that the children have been introduced to previously—by the teacher's direct instruction. The centers are not used to introduce new skills. They are sometimes referred to as *mastery centers* because their objective is to provide time and resources for the children to practice to the point that the essential skills, in particular skills of language and math, are mastered. That is, the skills enter long-term memory and don't have to be consciously called to mind each time the basic skill is needed.

The teacher would also tell you that the children need to be trained—before starting centers—in how to use the centers system and how to manage themselves in it. They need to know the appropriate ways to use the materials, to ask for help, and to record their work.

In some classrooms, you would see an adult volunteer or aide assist children in their centers work or one or two older students serve as tutors. With or without this kind of assistance, the teacher relies on a system of peer captains or co-captains, one for each center, to supervise the center activities. The children give and receive help from one another in relaxed and easy ways and show pleasure in being responsible for managing their own behavior and learning processes.

This centers approach to allowing one-on-one guided instruction is not just a good-sounding idea. It has been refined over a

25-year period, in all the elementary and middle school grades, and in different schools with very diverse student populations and budgets. We have seen teachers with various teaching styles adopt the centers system effectively. It is adaptable to the many ways that teachers conduct whole-group or small-group instruction. Nearly all who start the centers plan continue using it and declare that they would not want to teach without centers. We hope this book encourages many others to start them, too. It contains in detail all the steps to be followed and identifies the resources needed to begin successfully.

Many elementary classrooms today are not organized by guided reading groups but by whole-group reading instruction. As research is showing that many children require a close match between instruction and their individual skill levels, the necessity for modifying the whole-language approach to achieve the match is becoming clear. Some children just need more individual help in unlocking new words or other reading skills.

This centers system is designed to provide the match in skills practice—whether the teacher has been using homogeneous guided reading or the whole-language approach. What is required for the match is that the teacher identify specific skill needs of children who are having problems and provide direct, uninterrupted instruction and skill practice on those needs. For gifted students, the system also provides opportunities for the teacher to take them on to more challenging work.

Learning basic skills and using new concepts require practice. Practice work is essential, yet it is not generally being done well. The mastery centers system was designed to solve that problem. Practice work becomes more fun, more engaging, more efficient in giving feedback, and a better match to specific skill needs.

This book does not cover what the teacher does in the small group. Most teachers know exactly what they want to do in group time. Their concern is how to be sure that all the other children are working on currently needed skills—and working with materials on their own level—when they are not with the teacher. What we describe is how to set up a centers system to effectively manage the classroom while the teacher works with a small group.

2

WHY MASTERY CENTERS?

During a 32-year career one of the authors, Carolyn Lawrence, worked in 15 elementary schools and continues as a volunteer in tutoring children with reading difficulties. Linda Samek, another of the authors, is a long-time elementary teacher who is now specializing in math instruction for children who get stuck in learning math. In our careers, then as well as now, we see a disturbing pattern in children's responses to instruction. Children in the early grades seem to come to school eager, happy, and fully open to learning. Teachers of kindergarten and first- and second-grade students seem to experience less frustration in motivating children; they describe them as easier to handle and more spontaneously receptive to instruction. But by third or fourth grade, many children start resisting school. Some get bored, in particular with seatwork activities that involve mostly paper and pencil. The mastery centers described in this book, especially the centers with manipulative materials, were designed to sustain children's interest and eagerness in the practice work so essential to skill development. In this chapter, we describe what we have seen as the advantages of these centers over traditional seatwork.

CENTERS DEVOTED TO PRACTICE

Traditionally the term *center* has meant a place where children go to learn while the teacher is instructing other students. The learning centers that became popular in the late 1960s and 1970s were shown by research to be ineffective with some students. The students had trouble learning without the teacher's direct instruction and close monitoring. In this program, the term *mastery centers* is used to emphasize that the centers are for practicing essential skills, not for learning something new. Seatwork should be practice on skills already minimally understood and attained through the teacher's direct instruction. We know from research studies that such skill practice is essential until the skills become second nature.

The Necessity of Practice

By practicing basic language skills to a point of mastery—to the point that they are automatically used and do not require conscious processing each time—a child is ready for more complex learning tasks. Without this practice to mastery, some children experience confusion and gaps in their skills. The gaps become more serious as the children continue in the later grades.

High Interest, High Success

The challenge for teachers is to provide students with practice experiences that keep them engaged and refreshed. The centers system and materials described here have been tested and refined, with the objective of sustaining a high level of student interest. Research has shown that seatwork practice not only needs to hold students' attention but also should be designed for a high rate of success; seatwork is most effective when children can accomplish the work with 90% accuracy. That is the target for all mastery centers assignments. The teacher has to be sure that the materials are matched to the growing edge of the child's skills. Finding the match is not possible unless the teacher has taken care to find the instructional level of each child for each set of skills.[1]

Variety and Movement

Children enjoy the centers because they offer a more diverse environment in the classroom. Even though a quarter to a third of the centers contain paper and pencil work, the fact that the children change centers every 20 to 25 minutes stimulates them to work harder and more happily. This approach allows them to have more variety while the teacher works with guided reading teams or other small groups. While the quantity and quality of student seatwork is better in mastery centers, especially the manipulative centers, the children generally describe it as fun rather than work. We attribute this to the fact that the centers give them variety and a controlled way to talk and move about while they work.

More Data, Fewer Papers to Grade

From the teacher's viewpoint, the centers approach appears to offer no less or easier work than conducting the class with traditional seatwork. Teachers who already take the time to keep practice work matched to each child's skill level will find that the manipulative centers require no more time to maintain than traditional individualized instruction. In a few months, as the teacher continues gathering materials for the centers, he or she will find that the manipulative centers can actually save time if they are done correctly. Moreover, manipulative centers give the teacher more data about each child's instructional level and progress than conventional individualized seatwork does, and the data generated by the centers can simplify the checking of student work. This advantage comes from the self-feedback process of the centers. Students in centers actually produce more work, keep track of it themselves in a log, and get more feedback more quickly than they would through teacher-graded papers.

The Motivation of Self-Correction

Moreover, the immediate feedback provided by the centers activities is apparently more effective with many students, particularly with the children who take the teacher's feedback as criticism rather than as simple corrections. The self-corrective features of manipulative aids are experienced as a natural help for learning, and students continue with their work more smoothly without feeling emotionally unsettled. And when students are trained in peer coaching—before centers are started—the feedback received from a peer is also unlikely to dampen motivation.

Managing Time Well

Time in mastery centers is more structured than in the conventional form of seatwork. The children know they have a very definite amount of time in each center. When that time is up, they have one minute to clean their center and move to the next. In our experience with centers, we have found that children respond more positively even to assignments they don't like. The reason, we feel, is their awareness that they will soon change to another center. In our experience, children complete much more work successfully in the mastery center program than in the regular classroom during seatwork because of this structure. Also, we were pleased to learn that this structure has a valuable by-product. It trains primary-grade children about using time more wisely. They become more aware of telling time and of what time means.

Practice Matched to Reading Levels

Every classroom has children at different reading levels. Even those classes that are homogeneously grouped by ability can have three or more reading levels. Whether the teacher is using guided reading teams, integrated learning, the whole-language approach, or a thematic approach to reading, he or she needs to pull small groups to coach. This may be every day or a few times a week.

The centers in which children practice the reading and writing skills assigned to them on their particular level can have several children of several different levels working side by side without the children at the lower levels being stigmatized by their work being seen or heard by other students. The low- or high-achieving children are not frustrated by all the other centers because the tasks are self-adjusting and the students can function well at their own level.

Practice Matched to Learning Styles

Another important aspect of the program is that children's different learning preferences are being provided for by the use of the centers approach. The importance of different learning styles of children is being emphasized now in educational literature. With all the problems teachers have to solve, it is nearly impossible for teachers to provide specifically for the different learning preferences of all children. However, with a variety of materials put into the mastery centers, virtually all learning preferences are accommodated when the centers are in use.

For example, a large majority of students work better with sensory-rich learning materials. Reading to oneself involves only the sense of sight. Most centers materials involve more than one sense in the learning process. Moreover, teacher-led instruction involves a lot more listening than speaking. Many children do best when they can process their thoughts aloud instead of just listening, and the centers give them the opportunity to do that quietly. When you visit mastery centers in use, you will see children quietly talking to others or to themselves. Physical movement and socializing while working distinctly help some students learn better. When the children have been well prepared for working in centers, they know how to manage their movements and talking so as not to disturb others who prefer quiet for concentration and private mental processing. Addressing another kind of learning preference, the centers also provide for immediate, direct feedback on skill practice—a feature that is very important to some children.

Consistent With Research

The mastery centers approach incorporates many teaching practices found by researchers to be effective. To learn most effectively, a child must experience success many times each day. Centers are structured to provide work on each child's level. If a child doesn't understand a question or problem, he or she is encouraged to ask a peer for help. In this way, practice work is much more successful than it is in the isolation of paper and pencil work in traditional seatwork programs. Chapter 3 contains a summary of findings from research on teaching and relates these to features of the mastery centers program.

Teachers' Reasons for Using Mastery Centers

For a teacher who wants to revitalize a classroom that is experiencing burnout—either from the teacher or the students—the mastery centers approach is an alternative to regular classroom routines. Some teachers alternate between the two: traditional seatwork for two weeks and then mastery centers for about six weeks.

Some teachers, introduced to mastery centers, have chosen not to work with them. Typically, those teachers did not want any movement or whispering in their room during small group reading instruction. While observers usually are impressed with the quiet and self-disciplined way that students manage themselves in the centers, some teachers are distracted by the movement and voices of the students in the centers. Others have chosen not to use centers because they already have systems for varied activities that work well to engage children during the times the teacher is instructing the small groups. What do teachers who chose and continue to use mastery centers have in common? All of them have expressed concern about providing for students' differences in instructional levels and in having enough variety in seatwork to keep students engaged and interested. These concerns apparently gave teachers motivation enough to start mastery centers, and the results kept them using centers.

CONNECTING WITH CHILDREN

Attending to Mistakes

Teachers intend to provide successful experiences at the reading level of each child. When instructing in reading, especially in the primary grades, the active teacher is listening for hints of problems the students may have in the reading process. For example, as a child reads aloud, the first-grade teacher may discover that the child is pronouncing a word incorrectly because of not knowing the distinction between short and long vowel sounds. The teacher helps the child with a correction and makes a mental note that Jane had a problem with short vowel sounds. The teacher will tuck that information away (along with thousands of such pieces) and listen next time to Jane for the same error. Jane may need special help to correct the misconception she has about vowel sounds. First she has to unlearn the wrong behavior, then she has to be taught the right match of symbol to sound. The right sounds will be stressed generally in work given to Jane and perhaps to the whole class. When Jane opens her folder in the language skills center, she finds specific work on practicing the vowel sounds.

Every teacher, when listening to oral reading, wants to be alert to specific corrections children need, to help them read more effectively. This kind of special corrective feedback needs to go on all day, every day, in all the subjects that are taught—especially in written work where mistakes are not as obvious as in oral work. We have seen very successful teachers with most students but who did not connect with some of them on certain skills and concepts. Unless we spotted the gap or error, the student did not know what was needed, and the learning was blocked, uneven, or wrong. In some students, the confusions pile up, become frustrations, and lead to resistance to schoolwork. Staying so closely connected to each student's learning is hard work. We came to realize that effective teachers make frequent checks while teaching to be sure the children are internalizing what is being taught. Learning to check and connect takes time and practice, especially with students who bring with them a history of confusion and resistance.

MASTERY CENTERS ARE DESIGNED TO HELP WITH PROCESSING FOR INDIVIDUALS

Revealing Misconceptions

The self-correcting features of most centers allow children to make mistakes without embarrassment, find the problem, and correct it themselves or get feedback from a peer or adult helper. The mastery centers format seems to make it easier for students to ask for help when they feel stuck. In effect, they reveal more of their misconceptions and have better opportunities for corrective feedback. For the teacher who is determined to provide successful experiences for every student each day, mastery centers help.

Attending to Prerequisites

Another aspect of connecting with children's learning is being aware of the prerequisites needed in any learning situation. A child cannot learn a new skill without knowing the prerequisite skills. We like to use the analogy of a child's mind being like a brick house under construction. Several walls are being built at once, and they are in different stages of construction. One row of bricks in a wall may be the math facts involved in addition and may be five bricks high, while another row involving recognition of letters may be only one brick high. The teacher must know the status of each row of bricks in a child's mind if the next brick is to be put in the right place.

The pressure from state and school board mandates to move all children at the same pace through the prescribed curriculum results from a policy that ignores human nature and developmental differences in children of the same age. The pressure works against the need—obvious to most teachers—to give adequate attention to prerequisites. The teacher feels forced to get a unit of study covered and skips the process of checking to see if the child has the prerequisite concepts and skills. An example is a teacher asking a child to identify the noun in a sentence when the teacher has not checked to see if the student has the prerequisite understanding of what a sentence is—without which, identifying a noun will have no meaning whatsoever. This would be like asking a brick to hang in midair and sustain itself there. The materials we have used in mastery centers help the teacher be aware of prerequisite sequences.

When we started centers, we began by using what we knew the children needed for additional reading help, based on our observations of the reading teams. For instance, when we found children in a reading team who could not unlock a word because they lacked understanding of short vowel sounds, we would help them individually with the sounds during guided reading time. We also would have a short vowel chart to help them master the skills. When they seemed to have the sounds worked out—which could take several weeks—each of them would find, in the skills mastery center, a paper for practicing vowel sounds. We would check this paper on the same day we gave them the practice. As they needed it, we would continue to give them additional instruction on vowel sounds. Of course, this instruction could be done with the whole class in a review lesson, if needed.

Practice on skills that don't connect with a child's prior knowledge is futile and frustrating. But when mastery centers are planned correctly, they are places where children practice diligently to make perfect the skills they have attained but not mastered. By cementing skills each day, the children are ready for the next concept. Peer tutoring is very helpful in this kind of practice of skills. The tutor has often previously experienced the same difficulty and can relate to the struggle of the one being tutored. Tutoring is great for the tutors, too, because they are cementing their own skills as they do the coaching.

NOTE

1. Lawrence, C. M. (2004). *Literacy for All Children: A Formula for Leaving No Child Behind.* Lanham, MD: Scarecrow Education; Good, T. L., & Brophy, J. E. (2003). *Looking in Classrooms* (9th ed.). Boston: Allyn & Bacon. These provide an excellent and comprehensive review of the research on teaching and learning.

3

THE RESEARCH BASIS FOR MASTERY CENTERS

Mastery centers grew out of the practical need of improving the quality of seatwork. Their purpose is to make the practicing of skills more of a game than a chore. As mastery centers were refined, important findings from research on teaching were incorporated to improve the centers and the management of them. This chapter highlights the findings from the research and gives our answer to whether mastery centers are consistent with what research has revealed about effective classrooms.

Since the 1950s, researchers have been observing classrooms systematically to identify what works best to promote effective learning.[1] Their results have been encouraging. Today's educators have available from research a solid body of guidelines and techniques not available to previous generations of teachers. These findings from research are somewhat known in schools—but largely have not been well translated into practical procedures that all teachers recognize as the business of teaching. The mastery centers design is based on a careful review of the research on teaching. We believe it is a valid translation of key research findings into teaching practices that teachers can use comfortably and effectively.

THE SEATWORK PROBLEM

Most of a teacher's day is given to whole-class instruction toward required objectives. But children are not all on the same instructional level, and many of them need individual attention to stay in the flow of whole-class instruction. And the time the teacher takes for individual or small-group instruction means removing the large group from the immediate supervision of the teacher. Every teacher knows that some students do not work effectively without regular monitoring. One of the most important findings from research in classrooms is that *the least productive component of instruction is the relatively unmonitored time when students are doing seatwork.* Some have called seatwork a wasteland, referring mainly to the numbing effects of practice routines dominated by workbooks, exercise handouts, and other paper and pencil assignments.

Children's interest, active engagement, and productive time on task are at their lowest ebb during this kind of seatwork. The mastery centers have been designed specifically to deal with this problem. They provide for the managed practice of skills by the large group while the teacher is giving carefully matched instruction to a small group. Effective learning comes from the combination of three ingredients: whole-group instruction that is largely on everyone's level; the teacher coaching individuals and small groups so they can they can stay in the flow; and assigned, engaging practice work on each child's level.

FEATURES OF EFFECTIVE CLASSROOMS

Those who have carefully analyzed and synthesized the large body of research conducted in classrooms over the past 30 years have come to remarkable agreement on a set of features that are present in classrooms where students learn effectively. The features are described here because the mastery centers program has been designed to include as many of them as possible.

Time Allocated to Instruction

In effective classrooms, a high proportion of classroom time is actually spent on instruction, and downtime is avoided by good organization. *Downtime* refers to time spent on noninstructional activities, including housekeeping, taking roll, looking for and organizing materials, getting ready for lessons, the teacher's attending to interruptions (which consumes an amazing amount of time in some classrooms), and student socializing that has no instructional purpose. Researchers have observed some classrooms in which downtime takes up more time than actual instruction.

The organization and self-management habits that children learn in the mastery centers program minimize downtime—at the beginning of lessons, during centers work, and in the transition time between them. Mastery centers do not affect the total amount of time the teacher allocates daily to instruction, but they do help teachers limit the downtime.

Engagement of Interest and Attention

Effective teachers (we use this term to mean teachers whose students show measurable gains) organize and manage instruction so that students stay constructively engaged and attentive. Some years ago, researchers added the term *time on task* to the vocabulary about teaching and learning. Teachers do not need researchers to tell them that children may appear on task when they are not, or may be seriously concentrating when they appear to be daydreaming.

Students' time on task is clearly related to their achievement of lesson objectives. Even more closely related to achievement, but harder to measure, are self-confidence issues (addressed later in the chapter), students' genuine interest, and keen attention. Children's interest can be captivated by teachers' techniques and rewards, by their planning and organizing of engaging activities, and by their selecting attractive materials. But at some point, each child reserves his or her attention for whatever is personally, intrinsically interesting. The effective teacher has a variety of resources, techniques, and activities available that are likely to match the specific interests of students.

Researchers commonly report having observed classrooms where 70% or more of the students were "in neutral" (not attentive) for long stretches of time. This inattention was usually observed not only during seatwork time but also during whole-group instruction, particularly if the instruction was beyond the abilities of some of the children. In seatwork, the faster students tended to finish quickly and had no other assignment to engage them on their level, while other students gave up and were off task.

The most important research results regarding seatwork effectiveness, obtained by several different research methods, show that *students' persistent engagement in seatwork tasks*—obviously tasks on their own level of achievement—*is clearly associated with better general achievement over the course of the whole school year.* The mastery centers resources described in the other chapters have been well tested for engaging children's interest. Moreover, mastery centers are designed to provide variety in learning mode and content. Children know that if the first center of the day is not one of their favorites, the second or third one will be. Knowing they will shift to another center every 20 to 25 minutes helps them to stay attentive to things that are less interesting to them. They seem to take pleasure in the self-management that develops in this process.

Different Learning Tasks for Different Students

Fast, medium, or slow processing of information is only one of many student differences needing to be matched by different learning tasks. Instruction is more successful when adapted to students' personalities, learning preferences, and interests.

Mastery center materials are designed for a wider range of learning preferences and interests than are conventional practice materials. Individual centers do not appeal to the preferences of all students, but each student should feel confirmed in his or her preferences within the set of centers experienced in one day.

Staying attuned to a roomful of different personalities is a complex task for any teacher. Of course, some do it more naturally than others. However, teachers who use mastery centers report that observing their students' behavior in centers alerts them to more facets of a child's personality than they could have seen without centers work. The centers permit children to approach the learning activities in more individual styles than is possible in conventional seatwork. A teacher conducting a reading group can scan the room from time to time and spot behaviors that are indications of children's style differences in center activities. These add substantially to the teacher's store of knowledge about each child and give a more sensitive basis for adjustments of individual instruction.

Active Teaching

Research shows that effective teachers carry the instructional content to the students rather than relying on the curriculum materials to do so. They do not expect the textbooks to do the teaching by themselves. Nor do they expect students to get useful meaning from the materials without the teacher providing bridges and supports. For this reason, mastery centers are just for *practice* of skills and concepts that have already been introduced in active teaching. New objectives are not introduced in centers.

Another aspect of active teaching highlighted by research is the energy and interest demonstrated by the teacher and the conviction that the students can achieve. Starting mastery centers will not guarantee a teacher an infusion of energy or renewed interest in teaching, but it is likely to convey to students the attitude that this classroom supports active teaching and active learning.

Active Learning

When instruction is most effective, the teacher is providing multiple means for students to deal actively with material and is accommodating student learning differences. The teacher also has students actively interpret, use, and display their understandings so that confusions become visible and can be cleared up. This guideline from research was the primary one for the development of mastery centers.

Conventional seatwork mainly engages one sense: sight. And it requires the learner to become aware of the visual images of the abstract symbols of language and math on the printed page and to translate them into personal meaning. Irrespective of intelligence, this translation job is difficult, harder for some than it is for others. The perceiving and translating of symbols is helped a lot by multisensory experiences. Mastery centers are designed to be sensory rich and to provide physically engaging practice tasks through the use of manipulative learning aids, along with quiet talking and body movement in some centers.

Part of active learning is the process of managing one's own learning. The centers design helps students learn self-management in several ways, including maintaining a record of their activities for the day. The records make it possible for the teacher to see each student's progress and spot any confusion that needs attention. Researchers who have seen centers in action have all remarked on the ability of the children to manage their learning and behavior while in the centers.

Instructional Level

Research results favor heterogeneous classrooms, with students assigned to reading groups by reading level, to math groups by math achievement level, and occasionally to other groups by other criteria. A student's achievement depends upon having instructional materials matched to his or her level. Mastery centers help teachers manage the diversity of heterogeneous classrooms. The centers materials are graduated in difficulty and are self-pacing, so that when students are assigned appropriate materials in centers, they stay on level and are more focused.

Success Rate

Researchers agree that in whole-group instruction the effective teacher plans recitations and other teacher-guided tasks so that students have successful responses 70% to 80% of the time. Research also shows that effective seatwork and homework are planned for 90% success. These rates appear to be optimal for virtually all elementary students regardless of ability. The mastery centers materials we describe in this book are designed for a 90% success rate—and that can be accomplished when the teacher places the student correctly in the sequenced materials.

Pace

Researchers quite consistently find that the best pace through the curriculum and within special activities is brisk, with students working in small steps and at a high success rate, in continuous progress. These criteria apply to the selection of mastery centers materials. Of course, the centers materials are self-pacing, and their game-like qualities prompt students to move through them at as brisk a pace as is comfortable for them.

The Sequence of Practice, Application, Feedback, and Remediation

Following active instruction on new content, research shows that the effective teacher assigns individual practice, being sure each student knows what is expected and knows what to do and how to do it. The teacher then monitors student practice as needed, to ensure that the essentials are mastered to the point of overlearning. Remediation is the adapting of the curriculum to the student, *not* simply a repetition of previous instruction or a watering down.

Mastery centers are designed as part of this cycle, with the intent of making whole-group time more effective. When the teacher has taught a skill or new concept, a recap of the concept and practice in the skill are put in the centers folders, typically presented in different formats that make the practice work fresh. When students complete their individual practice assignments in the centers folders, the teacher has a way of monitoring what the individuals have learned and can adjust the next practice assignment accordingly. The self-monitoring features of the centers materials also save the teacher's time. The teacher then can use available time to help the students who need remediation that the adult or student aides cannot provide.

Research shows that student achievement is best in classrooms that have 20% to 50% of the day devoted to practice to overlearning that commits language and math essentials to long-term memory—in a setting that keeps children from being bored and that provides an enrichment kind of practice for faster students. Mastery centers were designed to provide that kind of setting.

Enhancing Positive Student Attitudes

The researchers identified the effective teacher as one who stimulates student ownership of learning by planning lessons that draw on the student's world outside the classroom, by stimulating student choices in projects, by teaching students to evaluate their own work, by planning for and expecting enjoyment in classroom activities, and by providing evenhanded treatment. Mastery centers fit the five criteria well.

Positive student attitudes depend in part on having materials and activities that bring some joy to classroom life. The design of centers and the materials selected for them aim at student enjoyment. They also aim at promoting all students' self-esteem as learners. There is nothing mushy or soft-headed about the objective of having students regard themselves as good learners. That's where the love of learning comes from.[2] And the essential condition for this objective is having work on one's own instructional level—work assigned and done in a way that avoids as much as possible the stigma often attached to the children whose level is lower or pace is slower. The centers materials are designed to accommodate many levels. Children working side by side in a center, apparently using identical materials, may be actually doing work at very different levels. The stigma of levels is minimized.

Friendly and Cooperative Environment

Researchers consistently found that in effective classrooms, the teacher is seen by students as supportive, enthusiastic, natural, and friendly and the teacher promotes these qualities in students. Cooperation is structured into the small-group work, peer tutoring, and informal helping, and these are part of classroom expectations and procedures. The teacher trains the students in ways of working cooperatively and provides coaching and reminders as needed. Researchers who have observed children at work in the mastery centers remark on the easy and friendly relationships they show in their work.

Management of Dialogue and Working Environment

The final general finding from the research in classrooms is that clarity, enthusiasm, purposefulness, and sound questioning skills characterize the effective teacher. (We find that teachers drawn to using the centers system typically have these qualities well developed.) Managing the work environment successfully includes structuring the physical environment to aid attentiveness and planning smooth transitions between activities. Mastery centers do not affect a teacher's style of conducting dialogue or other in instructional events outside of the centers. However, mastery centers are very much a part of the working environment and have a management system designed to help students be attentive to task and to make smooth transitions.

NOTES

1. Good, T. L., & Brophy, J. E. (2003). *Looking in Classrooms* (9th ed.). Boston: Allyn and Bacon. This is an excellent and comprehensive review of the research on teaching and learning.
2. Lawrence, C. M. (2004). *Literacy for All Children: A Formula for Leaving No Child Behind*. Lanham, MD: Scarecrow Education.

4

BASIC ORGANIZATION FOR MASTERY CENTERS

No one is surprised to see children absorbed in watching television or a movie for two hours or more. But to expect them to remain engrossed in schoolwork for even half that long without the teacher's direct supervision may seem unreasonable. But, in fact, it does happen daily for most students in classrooms using mastery centers. Good organization and planning make it possible. This chapter presents the broad picture of organizing for these centers. The subsequent two chapters give specific directions for planning and implementing centers.

CHAPTER 4

ORGANIZING FOR CENTERS

The Purposes of Centers Work

Practice work should always be planned and managed to serve its primary purpose: *successful* practice of skills and concepts that the teacher has already introduced to students in direction instruction. For most skills, the teacher needs to give each student enough time to master each skill—to overlearn it until it becomes familiar, automatic, and a part of the child's repertoire. Using mastery centers, the teacher plans the practice work, matches it to the levels of the children's reading skills—as identified in the guided reading times—and makes sure the assignments are finished in the centers. A daily check on the quantity and quality of completed work serves another primary purpose of mastery centers: to give the teacher data for connecting and adjusting instruction to each child. Incomplete or incorrect work signals the need for adjustment—revised practice work, remedial instruction, peer help, and so forth.

When practice is managed by mastery centers, most of the practice work is self-correcting and involves little paperwork. Typically, a student does paperwork in one center each day. The work in this center needs to be graded daily. Paper and pencil data are vital and cannot be replaced by the self-feedback of manipulative materials that produce no written record of the specific errors a child may be making. Paper and pencil data can become a part of a student's portfolio. More important, just by checking these papers daily, a teacher can quickly see the errors the child is making and teach him or her to correct those errors the next day in the guided reading team. There are other records in the manipulative centers, but these records are for letting the teacher know of a student's progress through the sequential manipulative materials and for signaling any changes needed to maintain the match of assignments to the students.

Saving Time to Plan

Centers take about three to four weeks of preparation, including time spent organizing materials and training the children. The time spent in preparation is rewarded by much more efficient learning of essential skills. In my (Carolyn Lawrence) school, where I was the assistant principal for instruction, I helped each teacher individually. We developed the materials for a class for approximately two 3-week periods, so the teacher could change out at least one manipulative center every three weeks to another group of materials. Sometimes we changed the center entirely to an art center, a science center, or just a quiet reading center. The main goal was to keep the children motivated and moving, step-by-step, in gaining skill mastery, with good self-esteem and enjoyment. The children are always pleased to find fresh materials in centers. They like the variety, and once they know how to operate in centers, they need little or no additional training.

Instruction Time

To begin mastery centers, the teacher needs to commit about an hour or an hour and a half to skill practice and guided reading during the instructional school day. The time devoted to this does not need be continuous. A teacher, for instance, may have two rotations of guided reading teams and centers before the children go to special area instruction, with the other guided reading teams and centers time coming after they return. The children rotate every 20 to 25 minutes through their reading team and three or four centers, continuously or not.

How Many Reading Teams?

Centers work most effectively in a self-contained classroom, using three or four different reading teams depending on the levels of the children and the class size. Initially, the teacher must decide how many reading teams to meet in a day. A teacher who has 25 students probably will need at least three reading teams. When the teacher has three reading teams, each child has three centers plus reading with the teacher each day, making a cycle of four components. On the following day, the child has three other centers plus the reading team with the teacher. So with three reading teams, a teacher maintains six centers.

A teacher with a larger number of children could have four reading teams, which would require a rotation of four centers a day for each student, plus a reading team. That can be done very successfully, and it reduces some of the frustrations that come with a larger class size. Maintaining four reading teams does take more time and energy but is worth the trouble if a teacher has a large developmental span in her classroom. If the teacher can adequately provide successful reading to each child every day with only three reading teams, this is a good place to start. But once familiar with the program, the teacher may want to shift to four reading teams and eight centers, which may be necessary with a larger class. It is important to remember that centers work best with only three to five children in each at one time. That is another factor in deciding whether to divide the class into four reading teams.

To illustrate the size of groups, suppose a teacher has 24 students, with three reading teams. When the teacher is working with a reading team of 9 students, the 15 others will be in centers, with an average of 5 students in each. Some reading teams are smaller or larger, depending on the spread of reading skill differences. If the number of students in a class is much beyond 24, the need for four reading teams and eight centers becomes obvious. We have seen teachers who only have two students in one of the reading teams.

Six to Eight Centers

The program described in this book includes eight centers. The centers are described briefly below, and in detail in the next chapter. A child experiences four centers on one day and four other centers on the following day—all of which are different except the paper and pencil center. That center contains work tailored to the child's particular skill needs not covered by the other centers.

Typically, centers are used only four days of the school week. As a principal, I urged my teachers to return to whole-group instruction on Fridays and give the children paperwork—some of it just for fun—and to give themselves time to check student seatwork or to give tests, do lesson plans, and get new materials ready. We told the children that Fridays were test days and we kept the papers for our records. That way, the children came to school on Fridays ready to concentrate on paperwork. The paperwork was not wasted, as it all pertained to skill mastery work the children needed. We also had a variety of games and puzzles they could do on Fridays. Even games and puzzles give very specific help in several skill areas. Friday was a time for the creativeness and preferences of each teacher.

What Resources Are at Hand?

When the number of reading teams and the time frame have been decided, it is time to look at materials available in the classroom. Usually, the materials already in the classroom are sufficient to begin the center program. Observing the process of centers in action and seeing what works and why, teachers develop ideas and criteria for selecting different kinds of materials. Chapters 5 and 7 contain suggestions for content in the centers and descriptions of resources that have proven effective in mastery centers. Chapter 7 also gives sources from which to purchase materials.

The Actual Centers

Centers A and E are actually one center devoted to language, arts, and paper and pencil work. This center, labeled with two letters (see chapter 7), contains traditional practice work the teacher would have required without centers. It consists of a container or file marked *A* and *E* that holds color-coded folders, one for each student. The color designates the group of students who rotate together through the centers—each child keeping the same color day to day. The center is labeled both *A* and *E* so that a student attending them on alternate days will have work in the skills center every day, work that is graded. Each folder contains work on the individual student's skill needs: duplicated sheets; workbook pages, suggested in the reading book's teacher's edition; or anything the teacher decides to check and grade.

Center B (and sometimes F) typically contains manipulative materials that are described and explained in chapters 5 and 7. The materials and content are quite varied, but all have in common sequenced skill practice with self-correcting feedback. Different manipulatives will be placed in center F if it is used.

For instance, when children complete each page with Versa-Tiles, they mark a record card, or if they are using Stepboards, each time they successfully put the pieces in a strip, they mark their record card.

The other four centers will contain various activities and materials, depending on the teacher's resources. Typically, one center can be for computer work, making use of the teacher's materials or software often provided in the school. The teacher selects programs that provide *practice* in skills already introduced directly by the teacher in whole-language, whole-group instruction or in guided reading team time.

Some teachers devote one center to writing. The authors used a writing center in many ways. Sometimes we put materials for making cards for someone or for doing a story about something we just experienced. With the current emphasis on writing skills, this is a center where a *teachable moment* can be the trigger for having students write what they think about a situation. An alternative to this center we used was a listening center, where students listen with headphones to books of their choice from the media center, or tapes that are especially developed to teach listening skills.

Another typical center is the potpourri center, or "this and that" center. It has the most varied materials, purchased or teacher-made. Teachers usually have a center for math skills practice, which may contain manipulatives, games for math practice, constructions, or paper and pencil worksheets. An arts and crafts center is commonly used, with materials changing frequently to provide variety as children complete one project and are ready to start another. Finally, a popular center used by many teachers is not actually a center but an opportunity to use the 25 minutes to go to the campus media center to browse and pick out books. Some teachers also have a quiet reading center, often a corner of the room where there are cushions for sitting on the floor to read to oneself.

Manipulatives Versus Paper and Pencil

Although manipulatives are a key factor in the success of the mastery centers program, the teacher does not need to be concerned with how many manipulative materials are available when beginning the program. Initially the children are enthusiastic just because of the novelty of moving to different activities in different places in the classroom every 20 to 25 minutes. There are other ways to start centers, without having work in them that requires grading; some of them are described in chapter 5. Manipulatives can be obtained as funds become available.

Some of them, including the ones recommended in this book, are relatively inexpensive.

When beginning centers, and throughout the use of them, it is important that the teacher not have more than one or two centers that have to be graded daily. More than two centers a day is too much of a burden for the teacher to handle in addition to maintaining the centers.

ESSENTIAL FEATURES OF ANY MASTERY CENTERS PROGRAM

Directions

Every center requires specific directions available to students at the specific site of that center. An example of directions for a paper and pencil center may look like this:

1. Get your folder from the captain, and a pencil if needed.
2. Do as much work in your folder as you can.
3. Mark your record card after each page.
4. Ask your captain if you need help.

We recommend using no more than three or four numbered directions for primary-grade students. In the manipulative centers, the directions will be similar, guiding the child through the pages of the booklet that contains the practice exercises. The students will have been trained in the mechanics of using each manipulative kit, so using it will be second nature and no printed directions will be needed for that.

The art center directions may look like this:

1. Get your folder from the captain and the art materials needed for your project.

2. Do as much work as you can.
3. Mark your record card when you finish.
4. Ask your captain if you need help.

Students Helping Students

There are several key points to remember when you are getting ready for centers. The students need to be trained not to depend on outside monitoring. While having some parents or tutors to help with centers is desirable, they are not necessary for an effective program. The children will develop responsibility for their work and behavior in centers if given appropriate training. They will also need some training in helping each other. Children helping children—peer tutoring—is one of the most effective teaching strategies that can be implemented in a classroom, once the children know what is expected of them. Interestingly, average children generally do better at tutoring lower-skill children than do the above-average children. The average students, having experienced the same learning frustrations as those they are tutoring, seem to have more empathy, patience, and understanding of what is needed to break through the difficulty.

The role of captain or co-captain is not reserved for above-average students. All students will take their turns as captain as the school year progresses. Suggestions for selecting captains and teaching students some basic helping skills are included in chapter 6.

Changing and Maintaining Centers

Another key factor to remember is that centers need to be changed periodically. While centers may remain constant as to the *kind* of work in them, a student's skill practice center is progressive, and the progression may continue over many weeks. A listening center may only need a change of books and audio materials as the student works through them; but the center needs to be replaced with an entirely different activity every three to four weeks. An art center only has to have new materials. The record cards or sheets in the manipulative center(s) are changed as students work through their assignments. In general, with the exception of the paper and pencil skills center, centers have about a three-week life span before the teacher must replace them with different kinds of activity or materials. Because the manipulative centers cover such a diversity of skills, the manipulative materials can be rotated back in after a three-week exclusion. The teacher should plan for changing one center every week or so to keep the centers motivational. Mastery centers are successful, in part, because the work is varied.

Recording and Monitoring

Paper and pencil skill center work must be graded daily. Also, it is important that these grades be recorded, much as traditional seatwork is graded and returned each day to students. Centers must be monitored to be sure that children keep record cards—when the teacher wants to have individual progress reports for the parents. Even if the children are only playing a game in a center, some kind of record should be kept. In the case of games or listening, the captain may keep the record for the group. The record keeping makes the children understand that each center activity they do is important, and they are accountable for what they do.

As these pages make evident, the mastery centers program is a system that has to be maintained to be effective. While it does not alter the majority of the classroom time and activity and does not affect a teacher's style of conducting whole-group instruction, it does change the 90 minutes or more devoted to small-group work, such as reading teams and seatwork. It calls for the teacher and students to learn and practice new habits and skills.

5

EIGHT CENTERS: OBJECTIVES, CONTENT, AND PROCESSES

A class needs to have twice as many mastery centers as guided reading teams. Thus a class with three reading teams will need at least six centers, and one with four teams will have eight centers. Here we describe eight centers. Teachers who decide to use six centers can still use the flow chart in the next chapter that depicts eight centers and condense it to six.

The sequence of the centers is important. What works best is having a sequence that alternates the centers that students regard as work with those they see as play. We describe the centers below in this alternating arrangement. All students will rotate through the centers in the same sequence; their homogeneous, color-designated groups just start at different places in the sequence. For example, the blue group could do centers A, B, C, D on Monday, then E, F, G, H on Tuesday, and back to A, B, C, D on Wednesday. The green group could start at center B and follow the same alphabetical sequence, and so on for the other eight color groups. Somewhere in the sequence, each child breaks out of it to be with the teacher in guided reading teams. The system is explained in detail in chapter 6. The eight centers described below, and the order of them, are just suggestions. Each teacher has to decide which centers to use, according to circumstances and the students' needs. After using centers for only a limited time, teachers become aware that the materials for centers are limitless.

The centers work well with the whole-language approach as well as in classrooms organized around guided reading teams. We recommend a combination of whole-language and reading teams—whole-language because it includes every subject every day and guided reading teams because they engage children on each one's correct instructional level until they are comfortable and confident in the reading process. This usually happens sometime in the fourth grade for average readers. Many if not most children from homes that give them rich exposure to reading in their early years can read with relative ease earlier.

All centers have six features in common. Each center has:

- a designation (letter, name, and perhaps a logo or identifying poster)
- color-coded folders with record sheets, one color per team and one for each student (In the arts and listening centers there is one folder for each group where the captain records the group's activity. In other centers the captains give out the individual folders to each child and they record their own progress. The folders typically hold the work to be done and a sheet for keeping a track of accomplishments.)
- something to hold the folders that the captain can manage: a bin, box, file, rack, or shelf (we used empty copy paper boxes and covered them with contact paper because they

were the right size for manila folders and they stack well
when not being used)

- a visible set of directions for each centers (see samples in
  chapter 4)
- all materials needed for functioning in the center
- a preassigned captain and a co-captain (for when the captain is in a reading team) who moves with his or her group

Centers A and E: Language Arts Skills
(Paper and Pencil) Center

As a general rule, as we said before, the objectives, content, and
processes of the language arts center are those the teacher would
have for conventional seatwork practices in language arts. This
may include whole-group instruction topics such as learning cap-
italization, writing, comprehension, fact and opinion, thematic
unit teaching, and so forth.

This is the one center that children use every day and the
teacher grades daily. When letter designations are used for centers,
this one would be identified as two centers, A and E. A child who
uses the center as A on Monday will use it as E on Tuesday. The
children's folders in this center may contain assignments from
their language arts book that the children read and respond to on
their own work papers, duplicated worksheets removed from a
workbook, copied materials from other sources, or copied blackline masters. It is very important that the work be matched to the
child's instructional level, so that he or she can complete each task
correctly about 90% of the time. The teacher grades and records
daily the work done in the skills center. If a child is reading below
level, the teacher may borrow a language arts book from a teacher
in a lower grade and find, for a particular child, the sections that
parallel the other children's books, but on a lower reading level. In
the teacher's manual of each reading series, as well as language

arts series, there are scope and sequence charts to follow that indicate which pages cover each topic.

Other worksheets used in the center, ideally, would come from the supplementary materials provided with the reading or whole-language series in use in the school—such as vocabulary work practice, comprehension exercises, and enrichment activities, which usually come in many forms, even some manipulative forms such as puppets. Every textbook publisher provides a comprehensive package of such resources, and many of the materials are an excellent fit for mastery centers. These materials should be put in the folders *after* the story has been taught—including a sequence where new words are introduced and comprehension questions answered—and the teacher has heard each child during guided reading. The teacher can check for use of the new vocabulary and be sure that the new material is on the correct instructional level for the child.

The graded papers are returned to the folders in the morning each day, Tuesday through Thursday, before centers time. The teacher may want to have a routine of sending selected papers home during the week to be signed and returned by the parents, while reserving some papers for the students' portfolios. If the graded papers are to be taken home from the folders each day, then this routine must be built into the directions for the center.

At the beginning of the week, the teacher will have prepared a week's work of materials for whole-group instruction, reading teams, and individual students' skill papers. When using separate guided reading teams, the teacher can anticipate how far each reading team will read in a week and have the appropriate supplemental practice sheets ready for each student's folder. This makes the centers and the whole process much more manageable.

Some students are helped considerably by visible symbols of progress. The record chart in the folder or the graded papers should give the child a visual record of completions, such as a bar chart. But giving the children the graded papers or a paper certificate of completion (award) usually thrills them, when they have consistently completed a large amount of work.

Careful selection of materials for centers A and E is very important. Because of mandates in instruction and curriculum from school boards, state governments, and the federal government, many teachers may not have been able to give specific reading instruction on the correct level of each child. The teacher has had to be too intent on getting an amount of content covered in a designated period of time. The teacher may not realize if the child is not ready for a concept. The materials used in the A and E centers help the teacher be aware of errors and misunderstandings that suggest missing prerequisite skills when the papers are graded each day.

Skill practice that does not connect with a child's prior knowledge is futile and frustrating for the child and is actually called the *frustration level* in reading. (There are three levels in learning to read: the *independent level*, which is where the child works with 90% to 100% accuracy; the *instructional level*, which is the match provided by the teacher introducing new material in small, incremental steps; and the *frustration level*, which is damaging because the student can't meaningfully accomplish the work being required.) By cementing the right skills each day, little steps at a time, the children are ready for the next level.

When we started centers, we began by using what we knew the children needed based on our observations in guided reading. For instance, when we found some children who could not unlock a word because they lacked understanding of short vowel sounds, concept clues, or configuration, we would help them individually with the sounds during the reading team. We would also put up a short-vowel chart in the room with pictures to represent the sounds (for example, *apple* for short a) and then put in their skills folders some words for practicing the use of these sounds. We would check their papers on the same day we gave them the practice. If they still were not clear about the sounds in the guided reading team, then we would continue to work on this skill as we incorporated it during the reading work or during the school day. Some children do not need specific instruction such as vowel sounds because they have mastered reading effectively.

Options for the Other Centers

If a teacher uses eight centers, there will be six in addition to the ones described above. The focus and composition of each one depends on what the teacher wants to emphasize at any given time. Here are descriptions of nine more centers that have worked very well. Whatever centers are chosen, they should be alternated in the work-and-play sequence described earlier.

Manipulatives Center

Many of the manipulatives we have used are like games to the students. Their game-like quality can be one of the criteria for selecting manipulatives, but the main criterion is skill development through concrete experience. Some teachers have a manipulative center each day, such as B and F. If two centers contain manipulatives, they will have different kits with different activities. Two sets of manipulatives were described in chapter 1: Stepboards and Versa-Tiles. There are other manipulatives that meet the criteria of being self-managing, self-correcting, devoted to skill practice and not to introducing new material, and being game-like so as to hold children's interest (see chapter 7).

Each manipulative kit has a very large inventory of practice booklets or cards, covering a wide range of objectives and content,

Table 5.1. Sample Record Cards

Versa-Tiles Record Sheet

Name _____

Book _____

1	2	3	4	5	6	7	8	9	10	11	12	13	14
15	16	17	18	19	20	21	22	23	24	25	26	27	28

Book _____

1	2	3	4	5	6	7	8	9	10	11	12	13	14
15	16	17	18	19	20	21	22	23	24	25	26	27	28

Stepboards Record Sheet: Language/Math

Name _____

Tile Color _____

1	2	3	4	5	6	7	8	9	10	11	12
13	14	15	16	17	18	19	20	21	22	23	24

Tile Color _____

1	2	3	4	5	6	7	8	9	10	11	12
13	14	15	16	17	18	19	20	21	22	23	24

GeoSafari Phonics Pad Record Sheet

Name _____

Date	Card Code	Card Score
_____	_____	_____
_____	_____	_____
_____	_____	_____

through many grade levels. The teacher will find skill practice materials that fit very well with any basic skills instruction program, particularly in language arts, math, and science. Teachers simply select the manipulative booklets, tiles, or cards that fit their lesson plans. While each manipulative kit provides for continuous skill development that could carry students through the school year, it is important to rotate the kits out of the center(s) every three weeks or so to provide variety.

The students learn how to use all the manipulatives in the training sessions that the teacher conducts before the children start using centers. They practice using them until they are certain how to use them, so that there will be no questions. Most children catch on quickly. If questions do arise during centers time, the captain handles them. Once the children have been trained in how to use each kit, they do not need additional written reminders of what to do with the manipulatives, and they don't need to consult the teacher. They simply have their folders that include an assignment of pages or cards to use and a log for recording their completions. In planning for the children's use of manipulatives, the teacher must decide where in the sequenced materials each child should start and write that in his or her center(s) folder. As mentioned before, these are self-pacing materials.

Quiet Reading Center

If the children have little in-school time for reading materials they choose for themselves, a reading corner makes a very good center and gives them at least 20 minutes every other day to read what they like, *not* what is required. Carpet samples and cushions on the floor to sit on—in a low-traffic area—make possible a good center.

Individualized Fun Skill-Books Center

This center is one that we have used extensively and that the children love. The books we use are relatively inexpensive paperbacks entitled *Homework Helpers*. They range in level from pre-K through the upper elementary grades in language arts, reading, and mathematics. The child writes in the book and keeps it when done—or it becomes part of his or her portfolio. The booklets present sequenced skill practice activities, with each page presenting a delightfully different activity. After finishing a page, the child picks out a reward sticker from the middle of the book and attaches it to the chart on the back of the book. The children truly enjoy marking their progress in this way.

The teacher can choose whatever books he or she wants that match the child's skill level. The grade level of the book is printed in the upper right corner of each book. So as not to embarrass children working below-grade level we always cut off the corner

or paste a label on top of it with the child's name. Because practice work is supposed to be done with 90% accuracy, it is extremely important that these booklets be matched to the child's independent level—a bit below the child's instructional level—so that they find the books fun and stimulating but not overly challenging. The children are assigned a few pages a day. Some teachers do grade these pages, and we think that that is a good idea. Other teachers simply have the captain record that the child has done the pages. Checking these pages gives the teacher clues to any skill gaps. (One of the authors recently graded a *Homework Helper* book and found that Ashley had not mastered the main idea of a paragraph. This concept had been taught many times. The clue from Ashley's pages pointed to the need to give her special help.) When a child completes an entire book, we give him or her a paper certificate of completion.

Of course, this is just one idea for the fun books. We especially like the *Homework Helper* books, but there are other materials that can be swapped for these.

Art Activity Center

Objectives and content of the art center may be drawn from any content area. The art activities can be extensions of study in the areas of art, science, math, reading, seasonal themes, music, physical education and nutritional themes, health and safety, current events, and social skills. These materials can be supplemental, for enrichment, or just for fun. Sometimes the art center is used just for children's exploration with materials. A wheeled art cart or containers that the children can easily carry will be needed. The cart should house all the art materials and classroom supplies likely to be needed: paper, markers, pencils, crayons, brushes, paints, rulers, scissors, glue, rubber cement, paste, stapler, and any other materials needed for specific projects.

Typically the art center will have one folder for each color group, not for each student. It will contain directions for the captain and may hold some kind of artwork in progress. The teacher monitors and maintains the center, daily or weekly, to keep the materials ahead of the children's use of them, and provides new written instructions and materials as the children shift to new projects.

The art center is a great opportunity for teachers to provide step-by-step directions that must be followed. Children follow the teacher's written directions as they construct a specific art project and produce a product. Some activities used by the authors are listed below as part of the math craft activities center.

Computer Center

Teachers who have computers in their room often find it useful to treat them as a mastery center. If pairing children together at a computer is necessary because of a scarcity of computers, the average child can actually help the developmentally low child better than an advantaged, above-average child. Research shows that the average child relates better and more easily to the below-average child. When computers are used this way, the teacher loads in programs that are just for practice of skills already introduced by the teacher. If work with computers is handled in a computer lab, with the whole class attending at one time, there are other options.

Media Center

We have successfully used this time slot to send children to the media center to browse, pick out a book, or read a book. When we do this, we send them with a timer, which is set for 20 to 25 minutes, for as long as the center time lasts. Children take library passes, something durable made of wood or plastic, so that a pass doesn't have to be filled out every time. The teacher will need to work out a permanent pass with the media center or principal or both. It is best if these passes can be hung on a rack or in some other prominent place, so the children know where to get them and return them quickly and quietly. For this center, there is one folder for the whole group, and the captain would just record how many went to the media center and if they were on task and orderly. The captain is also the timekeeper.

Potpourri Center

We like to have one center completely flexible as to objectives, content, and processes, with the emphasis on avoiding paper and pencil work. The content can be drawn from the entire curriculum. Here are some of the materials that have worked very successfully in the potpourri center:

- Picture puzzles, that is, small puzzles that can be done in 20 to 25 minutes if done by the group
- United States map picture puzzle for the group to do
- Games: math counting games, beads, or counting games with objects in a box
- Higher-level games such as Scrabble, Sequence, Racko, Take Ten, and Pigs (see chapter 7)
- Dot-to-Dot skills books
- Soma cubes or other materials that can be locked together

Listening Center

All children need to improve listening skills. These are skills that have to be taught. There are listening tapes available for identifying sounds, such as an airplane taking off, a motorcycle, and so forth. If the children have the ability, they could write down what they hear on a listening tape. In many instances, there may be some other listening technology in your classroom that you may want to use, such as books on tape, or some creative idea you have about listening skills. Typically, the content of the listening center is changed after two days.

Math Crafts Activities Center

Enrichment and challenge activities are often a good source of materials for centers. The art connection in math is strong and provides rich right-brain stimulation. Such projects are frequently eliminated from the instructional plan because of time constraints. Placing these activities in a center is an effective way of including them. The hands-on nature of arts and crafts assignments also provides the motivation that improves on-task behavior. Here are suggestions for activities that go beyond math facts to the concepts and mental operations that are the basis of mathematics.

1. Using graph paper and colored pencils or markers, the children write their names in large block letters and then calculate the area and perimeter of each letter.
2. Students build an abacus with cardboard, strung with pony beads, prior to instruction in how to use an abacus.
3. Students construct sets of solid figures from prepared paper sets.
4. The children make solid geometric figures out of clay.
5. Using flexible straws, students construct three-dimensional figures and identify the number of faces, edges, and vertices.
6. Given a picture with a grid drawn over it and a large-scale blank grid, the students practice making an enlarged scale drawing by completing individual sections of the final picture.
7. Using half of a paper cutout picture of an object, the children draw the missing half to make the picture symmetrical.

8. The students construct individual measuring tapes using floral wire and ¼-in. pony beads. Choosing two colors and stringing 48 beads, alternating colors every four beads, they make a 12-in. measuring tape. These can be used to measure assigned items. The self-made tapes make evident to children the meaning of quarter- and half-inch intervals. The tapes are also useful for addition and subtraction of fractions and for illustrating how to change improper fractions to mixed numbers.

9. The students create a tessellating shape—such as interlocking mosaic pieces—and then use multiples of the shape to cover a 9-in. by 12-in. sheet of construction paper, coloring it as desired.

10. The children build individualized glyphs, or carved figures. When their work is keyed to the seasons or instructional themes, their glyphs make great components for instructional bulletin boards.

11. Provided with copies of 100-charts, the children color factors for assigned numbers and describe the patterns that are revealed. They make a set (one for the 2s, 3s, 4s, and so forth) and staple together a booklet to use as a focal point to discuss patterns (both visual and numerical), symmetry, identifying prime numbers, and so forth.

12. The children are provided with a picture of an object that the teacher has enlarged and reduced so that there are five or six different sizes of the same picture. The students use nonstandard units (paper clips, cubes, mini-bears, crayons, erasers, and so forth) to measure each picture and record the length and width in those units. The picture that is enlarged and reduced might be an illustration related to a story currently being read or to a content area subject being studied—whales, rocket ships, and so forth.

13. Students make individual sets of tangrams from provided squares of paper and step-by-step directions for folding and cutting. The teacher supplies a few tangram pictures to challenge those who complete their tangram set. Many samples can be found on the World Wide Web.

14. The students create a map of an imaginary town using graph paper. The teacher can provide a key or allow them to design their own. Their instructions have them include mileage between structures or focal points and answer some questions regarding the distances traveled from site to site (some questions include round-trips). Once they have been introduced to the concepts, they could also be asked to describe locations with coordinates and movement between focal points using cardinal or intermediate directions.

Other Resources for Mastery Centers

As we have said, most schools already have excellent materials, often labeled as remedial or enrichment skill materials, which are included in the package of resources that textbook publishers supply when the school adopts subject matter texts or whole-language or phonics-based reading programs. It is surprising how often these resources are overlooked—in much the same way that some teachers, so pressed for time to meet curriculum obligations, do not use the rich resources of the teacher's edition as they teach. Besides excellent ideas for skill practice activities, these neglected resources include some excellent posters, puppets, charts, hands-on construction plans, that are so useful in mastery skills centers and in manipulative centers. The blackline masters of remedial and enrichment activities are especially good for centers. The teacher can select from them the ones that match what has been taught in whole-group instruction or in guided reading teams in previous weeks and now can guide skill practice and reinforcement in center work.

The pressure on teachers to cover the curriculum is a very real force in today's schools. The centers format provides an effective antidote to the pressure. It provides a time-efficient way to get these rich resources into the hands of the students. Two of these authors admit that we had many unused materials given to us when we changed or adopted a new text in subject areas, including reading. Personally, we always felt guilty about throwing away any of these materials but could not get to them. Now a teacher can use at least some of them.

Once a teacher gets the knack of using mastery centers, there are literally hundreds of materials a teacher can use in the centers with flexible content: comic strips (cut up) to put back together for sequencing in a story, puzzles, games, coin cards that must be put together to match, and so forth. Quiet reading of fun books, comic books, games—all are encouraged for at least one segment of the centers cycle each day. The activities selected have to meet a few simple rules: children have to be able to manage the materials themselves; the materials need to be numbered so the students can do one after the other with a record card; the materials must be on the children's level; and fourth, they have to serve instructional objectives and be worthy of the children's time.

6

STARTING
MASTERY CENTERS

We would like to emphasize here that professionals in teaching have been using centers for years. This program can be, and should be, modified to fit a rotation with which the teacher feels comfortable and which is already working well in the classroom. But in order to provide for individual levels of the students, keep adequate records, and thus give more motivation to the students, we are suggesting that the basic recommendations be included in your centers program. The basic guidelines are discussed in chapter 5 and are summarized here:

1. Assign each child seatwork on his or her correct instructional level, to attain at least 90% correct answers.
2. Sequence the centers so that what the children perceive as play centers alternates with centers that appear to them as being homework or schoolwork.

3. Look for and use manipulatives as you can find them or purchase them and *always* have a record card for each child.

4. Create, organize, and practice the centers many weeks before you start them. Be sure the children know exactly what they are to do, how to record their progress, and how to work and clean up the centers after use within one minute. They must be specifically trained for cleanliness and orderliness. (To make the transition quiet and orderly, we trained the students to follow an added rule during the changing-centers minute: move to the next center without speaking to or touching one another.) As children become used to a high standard of work and record keeping in their centers, they will become more oriented to peer tutoring and more accustomed to leaving the teacher alone while a small guided group is being instructed.

5. Remove centers and change them as student engagement with them starts to wane—in general, about every three weeks.

In addition to planning the content and procedures in each of the centers, as described in chapter 5, four other aspects of the program must be planned before starting centers work: the grouping of students, the system for movement through the centers, preparing the students, and arranging the classroom. Described below is the way we trained several hundred teachers, most of whom continue to use the program in their own way at the present time.

Grouping Student for Mastery Centers

When the teacher is using a guided reading team program, each student will be a member of two groups: a reading team composed of students at basically the same reading level; and a mastery centers group, designated by a color and composed of stu-

dents of varying ability and achievement levels. We use the word
team for the reading group to deemphasize the fact of ability
grouping and to minimize the stigma often attached to being in a
lower-level group. During guided reading centers time, when they
are not with their reading team receiving instruction from the
teacher, students will be in centers with their color group.

We use a systematic mixing of students in forming the color
groups. First, we list numerically all the students in the class, entering as number 1 the name of the strongest student (on the basis of academic and leadership skills). We continue to list students, ending with the weakest student. We use the list to form
the color groups, as shown in example 6.1. This example, using 30
students and eight color groups, results in three or four students
per color group. Continuing with this example, we will assume
that there are four reading teams.

The color system can be used for movement through the centers. The eight colors noted in the example can be arranged on the
charts to tell the students which center to be in at any given time
(see example 6.2).

The charts appear complicated at first glance, but once the system is explained to them and they practice it, the children have
no difficulty with them. Examine the charts line by line. On the
first color line, note the color pattern: red, yellow, purple, green,
orange, brown, pink, and blue. The order of colors stays the same:
for example, purple is always after yellow and before green. The
color that ends the first line begins the second, and so on.

The charts can be made so that each color line relates to the
number of a guided reading team. The rule the children learn is
that when Team 1 is with the teacher for reading, the first line of
the chart shows what color group goes to which mastery center;
for example, the red group goes to center A, the yellow group to
center B, and so on. Note that each group goes through the centers in alphabetical order. Red, for example, goes to A, B, C, and

Class roster, sorted by skills level:

1. Sam Strong
2. Suzanne almost as Strong
3. Ashley Able
4. Andy almost as Able
5. And so forth

Color groups:

RED	YELLOW	PURPLE	GREEN
1. Sam	2. Suzanne	3. Ashley	4. Andy
9.	10.	11.	12.
17.	18.	19.	20.
25.	26.	27.	28.
ORANGE	**BROWN**	**PINK**	**BLUE**
5.	6.	7.	8.
13.	14.	15.	16.
21.	22.	23.	24.
29.	30.		

Example 6.1

D on the first day, and E, F, G, and H on the second day. Yellow's rotation starts with B. Some teachers attach a clothespin to the left side of the chart and move it from line to line to remind the students which segment is starting.

Day 1	A	B	C	D	E	F	G	H
Team 1	red	yellow	purple	green	orange	brown	pink	blue
Team 2	blue	red	yellow	purple	green	orange	brown	pink
Team 3	pink	blue	red	yellow	purple	green	orange	brown
Team 4	brown	pink	blue	red	yellow	purple	green	orange
Make-Up 5	A	B	C	D	E	F	G	H

Day 2	A	B	C	D	E	F	G	H
Team 1	orange	brown	pink	blue	red	yellow	purple	green
Team 2	green	orange	brown	pink	blue	red	yellow	purple
Team 3	purple	green	orange	brown	pink	blue	red	yellow
Team 4	yellow	purple	green	orange	brown	pink	blue	red
Make-Up 5	A	B	C	D	E	F	G	H

Example 6.2

The last part about the charts that we teach the students is that they leave their color group when it is time for their reading team to be with the teacher. Because of the way students were assigned to color groups—carefully mixed in terms of ability, achievement, and leadership—a homogeneous reading team will have a child from virtually every color group.

Thus, during Team 1's time to be with the teacher, all members of that team leave their color group for reading instruction; they rejoin the color group in the next time period. The bottom line of each chart, the fifth time period, can be a time for makeup. This is the time students make up center work missed during small-group reading instruction.

Because the teacher does not have a reading team during the fifth time period, he or she is free to monitor the centers work or to give individual attention to students who need special help.

Preparing the Students for Mastery Centers

Preparing a class for mastery centers should begin three to four weeks before actual implementation of centers. During the preliminary time, the teacher is:

1. Collecting and organizing materials for the centers.
2. Establishing record keeping for the various activities.
3. Training the students to operate equipment and manage materials. All children will know the captain's and co-captain's jobs. The first ones to be captains will not always be the captains; others will have the job as they show themselves able to do it. We suggest that a child in each color group be designated a co-captain, to take the responsibility when the captain is pulled from the group to have reading instruction with the teacher or when the captain is absent.
4. Training peer tutors and adult volunteers.

5. Deciding on reading teams and color groups.
6. Training the students to understand the charts and how to move from center to center.

The preparation tasks listed as 1 and 2 above have already been described. Some of the training of students to operate equipment and manage materials can be done in whole-group instruction, and some must be done with small groups. When the teacher needs to train some students in small groups, the remaining students need to be engaged in something that does not require the teacher's attention. For example, they can be doing their skills seatwork using their individual color-coded folders. An alternative is to have the large group read comic books or other things they choose to read.

During this training time, the teacher works in the centers and not with a reading team. If the teacher needs evidence of leadership skills and cooperation patterns, for purposes of placing students in color groups, these two or three weeks of training with small groups usually will give the data needed. Also, this is the time for training student tutors and adult volunteers or aides. They learn along with the children and may need some additional coaching away from the children. As noted before, tutors and aides are not essential to the program, but the teacher may want to add them after the children are managing the centers.

The steps for deciding on teams for guided reading and color groups have already been described. Showing students what a color group means can be done simply by using eight sheets of paper or cardboard in the color of each of the eight groups. The name of the color is written on the top of the sheet, followed by the group members' names. The captain can take the sheets to the center at the time of changing the center. During the first few weeks, color-coded name tags for each child will help the teacher be sure that each is in the right center. The teacher should stay in the centers and not begin reading instruction until the centers are working smoothly.

The students also need to be trained to move between centers in an orderly way. What we call the *three-bell system* works very well in managing quiet and smooth transitions. The teacher keeps track of time, of course. Some prefer to set a timer, such as a kitchen timer. We have seen children respond favorably to the timer by staying on task when it is ticking. When the timer rings, it is the first bell in the three-bell sequence.

The first bell means clean up the center and sit quietly. The teacher looks to see that all centers are ready for changing, then rings the second bell. That is the signal to stand, look at the chart, and locate the next center. When all are quiet and ready, the third bell is sounded and the students move to the next center. The teacher then resets the timer, and no one has to be a clock watcher. When the teacher wants to lengthen or shorten the reading lesson with a particular team, the timer can be moved slightly back or forward. We recommend 20 to 25 minutes for each reading centers segment.

Students can be taught about the charts line by line in much the same say they were explained in the previous section. The children quickly become comfortable with the charts and the process of changing centers. They enjoy the self-management it entails and take the responsibility seriously if the teacher sets the right tone.

Arranging the Classroom for Centers

Usually teachers using centers have student desks already arranged so that no movement of furniture is necessary for centers time. Students just clear their desks. The materials for a center should be in a box or other container the children can easily carry to the center.

In large classrooms, where centers are separate from students' desks, the centers tables are located close to the shelves, cabinets, or tables that hold the materials to be used in the respective centers. Many teachers can arrange centers so that no desks or tables need to be moved. In classrooms where some furniture needs to be moved for centers time, strips of colored tape are sometimes placed on the floor to designate where furniture is to be placed during whole-group time and during centers time.

The table or floor space for reading instruction should permanently be arranged so that all the reading team members can easily see the teacher and have their backs to the students in centers. The teacher is positioned so as to see all the students in the room.

The centers charts are hung where they can be seen easily from any position in the room. The colored sheets listing color group members and lists of reading team membership should be posted near the charts. Signs designating the location of centers are often hung from the ceiling over the centers.

Checklist prior to starting centers:

1. Are the center charts up?
2. Are the reading teams assigned?
3. Are the color groups assigned? With captains and co-captains?
4. Is the room arranged for centers?
5. Are there signs up to designate centers?
6. Is record keeping established?
7. Are name tags made?
8. Were students instructed in care and use of materials?
9. Are materials in the centers?
10. Have students practiced moving from center to center?

7

RESOURCES FOR
MASTERY CENTERS

Listed in this chapter are manipulative kits and other materials that have proven highly motivational and effective in mastery centers. The manipulative hardware is durable and the companion booklets and cards can be used many times. We continue to use some of the same materials, specifically Stepboards and Versa-Tiles, 20 years after we purchased them. The authors receive no compensation for listing any of these materials. All of the materials listed have been used by the authors, however, and some companies sent them free to us for perusal. We are just alerting readers to resources we have found to be successful.

There are many familiar and common materials, such as games, puzzles, art materials, connect-the-dots booklets, and so forth that work very well in mastery centers. We are not describing them here because they are readily available at school supply stores or discount stores locally. Just a cursory inspection of the materials will show which ones meet the criteria for mastery centers: self-managing, game-like, with self-correcting instant feedback—and appropriate to the curriculum. Only a few of the materials come with record cards or other means for children to chart their completions. The teacher must construct record cards or sheets for each center. They are a vital component for the children to take the games seriously and the teacher to follow the children's progress.

Several teachers may want to purchase these materials collectively and form a school manipulatives center where materials are catalogued and checked out. Pooled monies from grade level or school budgets are a common way to start. The authors equipped a manipulatives center with some of the monies from a $20,000 grant written for a specific elementary school. With the help of the media specialist and volunteers, the teachers had ready access to materials to change centers as often as needed. We found this to be successful in saving time for the teachers. However, a checkout system had to be developed and all teachers had to adhere to the policies for the manipulatives center to work effectively. We also found that one person had to monitor these materials weekly for breakage, battery recharging, and other upkeep. Sometimes the media specialist will do it. The teachers can also share this job on a rotating basis, so no one person is stuck with the responsibility.

Pooling funds and having a resources center make possible the purchase of more varied manipulative hardware materials and a more in-depth inventory of companion booklets and work cards. New resources can be added gradually to the center as funds become available. It can be set up for all teachers in the school to use or just for a particular grade level, or just for the primary-grades teachers. We have seen all these options work successfully.

INSTA-LEARN STEPBOARDS: BASIC SKILLS MATH, READING, AND VISUAL PERCEPTION MANIPULATIVES

The Insta-Learn system provides a multisensory approach to practicing basic reading, math, and perceptual skills. The immediate feedback to the child allows individuals to work at their own pace and level. If a tile is put in incorrectly, it will not fit, and the child can change without any correction from the teacher, peer, or volunteer. The children can build their confidence by correcting the tiles immediately.

Each board is a 13-inch-by-19-inch plastic frame with 26 pieces for both upper- and lowercase letters. The basic number boards are the same size and range for counting from 1 to 25, but they accommodate practice from 1 to 100. Also, there are boards in multiplication and division.

The 26 two-inch-square pieces are notched at the bottom, making it impossible to complete an answer without the correct letter piece. There are 24 program strips to each practice section, providing variations on the same skill. The teacher selects program strips that the child puts into place (one at a time) at the bottom of the board, following the quiz items in the companion booklet.

The strips in language arts range from perceptual skills such as recognizing letters, numbers, and basic counting and graduate to include long- and short-vowel sounds, comprehension, sequencing, and all skills needed for encoding and decoding words. The grade levels range from kindergarten to fourth grade. The strips in math range from matching numbers and dots (one-to-one correspondence), simple word problems, simple addition, and double addition and subtraction to multiplication and division facts and word problems in fourth grade.

The teacher needs to make two additions to the provided materials. Some of the strip sets have pictures on them for the children to identify and then spell the names of them. Some pictures could represent several things and may confuse some students. For example, one strip shows a picture of a swing, a teeter totter, a slide, and a tree, all clustered together. Four letters make up the answer that will fit on top of the strip. The letters that fit spell *park*, not *play*, one equally feasible choice. Wanting the children to be clear about what word they are trying to spell, we made photocopies of the strips with pictures of possibly confusing or unfamiliar items and went over the pictures with the whole class to identify what words the pictures represented. Six strips will fit on one photocopy sheet. Of course, the teacher may prefer to tell the children that they have to solve the mystery of a picture by trying different puzzle pieces. But first-grade children especially need coaching on a few pictures, which can be done by a volunteer at the center.

The second addition to be made is a record card and folder for the child to mark when each strip is completed. See the sample card in table 5.1. When all 24 strips are completed, we give the child a certificate or reward. Information for this system can be found at www.insta-learn.com.

GEOSAFARI PHONICS PAD

This is a very exciting, inexpensive reading program with 128 interactive cards that use a touch-system pad. The child can touch the pad and get feedback by way of a voice and flashing lights in a systematic and fun way. We have found this to be very motivational. Children are assigned a specific set of multicolored cards that give them practice in numerous skills—such as long- and short-vowel sounds, rhyming words, and reading simple sentences—that match their needs. (Earphones are possible.) The phonics pad may be used separately or with peers in a mastery center. We don't think more than two children should be at one phonics pad.

GEOSAFARI LAPTOP

This is an exciting game that has wonderful, award-winning lesson cards. The lights and sounds guide the game play for different skills and provide feedback to each child. (It can be used with earphones.) It has self-storage for 63 cards and three different modes of play. Although we have used it only for individuals one at a time, it can easily be adapted to two to three players helping one another or playing one at a time for 30 to 60 seconds. The laptop requires four AA batteries and includes grade levels from kindergarten through at least ninth grade. The hardware comes

with 63 two-sided lesson cards for grades 3 and up, covering skills practice on science, language, math, and history. There is an expansion kit of 63 cards on basic skills for pre-K to grade 2.

GEOSAFARI

This electronic upright frame and keyboard initially came with cards focused on geography. Now it has 20-card sets on many topics, including dinosaurs, wildlife, history, sports, word power, and many more topics. It is interactive with self-checking quiz games like the two described previously and is very popular and effective. The card sets provide skills practice in many curriculum areas. GeoSafari includes automatic answer, correction, and scoring. It is used with batteries or an AC adapter and may be used with headphones. Children in all grades, especially grades 3 and up, love to do these games by themselves or in a group of two or more;

the group investigation adds impetus. As with other manipulatives, these materials require the teacher to make record cards. We use these materials ourselves and have observed them in use in diverse classrooms. We can enthusiastically say that these materials are effective for exceptional student education as well as regular classrooms, and all children appear to love the autonomy of investigating on their own or together. They learn much more that just the subject matter. Information about this can be obtained at www.educationalinsights.com.

VERSA-TILES

Versa-Tiles is a self-corrective drill-and-practice learning system that promotes skills mastery in language arts, reading, math, life skills, and science as well as other subjects. Problems are solved by placing tiles, corresponding to the question number in the booklet, on lettered answer spaces in each case. Exercises are instantly self-corrective by closing the answer case, turning it over, and checking the colored pattern formed on the back of the tiles. The child knows the answers are correct when the geometric pattern matches the one printed on each exercise page. The Versa-Tiles 30-page booklets contain sequential skills questions that build reinforcement with each exercise for grades K through 8.

We have used Versa-Tiles for many, many years. It is very important that the children have been trained and know exactly how to use them. We introduced the Versa-Tiles to an entire class several times, with all the children looking at the same page copied from one of the booklets, so they would understand exactly what to do. The children were taught that when the pattern is not correct, they must pick out the wrong pieces, turn over the tile box, and redo ones missed. As always, the teacher needs to make a record card or sheet for the child to fill out when a page is completed. We give recognition when a book is finished. More information can be obtained from www.versa-tiles.com. See sample in table 5.1.

READING MANIPULATIVES

We found these simple manipulatives—innovative, reusable laminated strips—to be very useful. The materials involve students working together and giving immediate feedback. Because children are performing at many levels, these manipulatives can be sorted as skill sets and put into plastic bags for each child to read to another child.

With compound words, for example, the first part of the word on the laminated flip-strip can be folded under. The child reads the core word and then opens it up to reveal how another word, a compound word, is added by the other part of the strip. These mastery skills materials work well in a center because the children take turns holding the strips for each other while one child reads.

We would put each group of skills in the plastic bags that are included. The teacher picks out the group of skills—that is, compound words, prefixes, or suffixes—and assigns them to a child or children in the group. If they are being used by a group, we think only one record card is needed for the entire center; the captain marks off that each child has read the materials. The teacher should be sure children know the skills before the set of strips is put into the center because the work in centers is practicing to mastery of skills already taught by the teacher. More information can be found at www.readingmanipulatives.com.

OTHER SUGGESTIONS

Custom-made books, such as the coloring book *A World of Orchids* by Deborah Cohen of Gainesville, Florida, represent another kind of resource—books that can be custom-made for whole schools or a school district to teach materials in a certain unit of study. This booklet was produced for a special unit done on flowers. It was chosen, from many other titles, to provide an example of what can be done.

Many communities have talented resource people, like Cohen, on whom teachers can draw. Sometimes the author or artist can come to the classroom. Needless to say, the children are delighted to engage in a dialogue with creative people.

Games

All teachers know of educational games. Those we listed in chapter 5 are described in detail at www.centralconnector.com/Games/html.

8

MASTERY CENTERS AND PROFESSIONAL INTELLIGENCE: RESEARCH IN ONE SCHOOL

By Rodman B. Webb, professor, University of Florida

In 1929, John Dewey discussed some of the impediments to developing a science of education. He looked forward to the day when teachers could consult research findings to aid them in decision making. Science, he said, would never tell teachers exactly what to do, but as knowledge accumulated about teaching, science could suggest things for teachers to try. In other words, science would never replace teachers' own intelligence, but it could inform them, give them ideas, help them do a better job, and make them more reflective in their work.

The science of education would be impossible, Dewey said, if it ignored the real, everyday problems teachers face and the solutions they devise for solving those problems. There was a need to investigate and enlarge upon the practical wisdom of classroom teachers. In Dewey's scheme, researchers and teachers would form an alliance in which they share perspectives, insights, and expertise.

A number of us at the University of Florida have been influenced by Dewey's concept of research and teaching. Thus, when Carolyn Burkett (now Carolyn Lawrence) called to see if we would be interested in doing an ethnographic evaluation of a program she had designed with teachers, Elizabeth Bondy and I were eager to participate. The two of us spent a total of 28 hours at the school, observing in classrooms; interviewing teachers, administrators, and parent volunteers; and looking over curriculum materials. We generated more than 80 pages of fieldnotes and analyzed the data using a modified version of Spradley's ethnographic method. Our findings are not definitive, but they are suggestive and encouraging.

Programs do not exist on paper, they exist in action. Thus, the bulk of our time was spent observing in the classrooms. We knew the problems the program had been designed to solve:

1. Teachers needed uninterrupted quality time to teach small groups of children.
2. Students needed uninterrupted quality time to practice what they learned in small-group and large-group instruction.
3. It was assumed that practice would be most beneficial if

    *   children could get immediate help if they were having difficulty
    *   children's work was corrected immediately, as it was completed
    *   practice exercises addressed a variety of learning styles and learning levels
    *   manipulatives, games, computers, and teaching machines augmented traditional worksheets
    *   activities were interesting and relatively brief

As every educator knows, it is one thing to list objectives and quite another to meet them. The researchers' task was to see if the goals that were set for the program in fact were being met. Our findings were clear on this point. Our data showed that the program *provided a mechanism that helped teachers accomplish each of the objectives listed above.*

When observing in classrooms, we were immediately struck by their quiet orderliness. Students were generally on task and interested. In addition, they displayed an impressive degree of cooperation. They worked in heterogeneous groups, monitored one another's behavior, and gave assistance to their classmates. Classes were extraordinarily independent, generally requiring little monitoring or help from the teacher. Even first- and second-graders worked with quiet efficiency.

We did several time-on-task checks in which we tried to assess the behavior of the children in the classroom. At no time were more than five or six children off task, and seldom was off-task behavior disruptive. Two excerpts from my fieldnotes describe some typical events:

> Children often whisper quietly to themselves as they read instructions from the worksheets. When two children begin talking together, a fellow student asks them to be quiet.

> A student looks over her work and comments to no one in particular, "Wait a minute, I messed up." She frowns and reviews her work and then looks over to the paper of the student next to her. "What's that?" she asks. Her neighbor gets up and looks at the first student's work. He offers a few words of explanation, then sits back down.
>   The girl works on. And another boy gets up and goes to the teacher to ask a question. The teacher asks, "Did you ask Stacy or Tracy?" He returns to the table and asks Stacy to read a difficult word for him.

Students in every classroom were free to talk quietly, move around the room, and ask for and give assistance. There was an atmosphere of industry and cooperation in all classes we observed. If the noise level began to build, or if off-task behavior began to get out of hand (though we did not see this happen very often), the teacher brought things back to normal with a friendly reminder.

We did not investigate children's perceptions of the program, but their industry and concentration indicate that they did not find the program onerous. Teachers in most classrooms returned to full-time whole-group instruction every six or seven weeks. Longer periods, the teachers claimed, taxed their students' endurance and lessened the program's effectiveness. Experience taught teachers that after about six weeks, the benefits of the program began to diminish. Students did not cooperate as comfortably, competition emerged, and the drive to complete assigned tasks led some students to copy from their neighbors. The negative effects were avoided, however, when teachers returned to traditional whole-group instruction for two weeks or so.

We observed numerous incidents of students monitoring one another's activities and offering assistance. We observed very few incidents of conflict. Typically, children went directly to their assigned centers, took out their folders, read the instructions, figured out what needed to be done, and set out to complete the assigned activity. While they worked, they frequently spoke softly to themselves. These verbal demonstrations of concentration were not disruptive. Occasionally, students would talk with their tablemates about nonschool matters, but these discussions were quiet and seldom lasted long. Children would drift from work into conversation and back to work in a pattern that reminds me of how my wife and I work when we share an office. Here are some examples of some typical center behavior excerpted from fieldnotes:

> The teacher calls class to attention by hitting a steel triangle. She tells the children to check the chart to remind themselves where they must go. She taps the triangle again, and the children move.

Some children assemble around the table by the teacher's desk. The other children break into small groups of twos and threes and proceed to their centers. I stand by center D as two boys and a girl select their folders from the display area and quietly sit down at the table. They open their folders and spread the contents before them. The folders contain two packets of stapled sheets. All of the sheets are devoted to letter sounds and blends. Most have to do with the *st* sound, but there are some *m* sounds on one sheet.

The children go quickly to work. They display an odd combination of attentiveness and oblivion. They are attentive to their work and will talk quietly to themselves as they solve the problems presented to them on the worksheets. They are also attentive to one another and remain at least peripherally aware of what other students at the table are doing and how quickly and/or accurately they are proceeding. They are attentive to the self-talk of their tablemates but pay little attention to what students are doing at other tables.

I'm reminded of the contextual nature of communication. Students who seem oblivious of one another will abruptly begin a conversation that is only possible because they have given attention to one another's work. To the observer who is not sharing the worksheet experience, the spontaneous conversations seem as miraculous as they are confusing.

Students at center D are working quietly. Robert looks up and says to Becky in a corrective tone, "You don't need two." Becky answers, "Yes, I need another." The interchange appears to refer to something Robert has written on his worksheet. Robert ends his participation as abruptly as he began it and recedes into self-talk: "Stop," he says, still working on his blends, "st, st, stop, st, stop."

At the same time, another student is whispering as he works: "Mommy, m m m m, Mommy, m, m, monkey." The small boy's brow is furrowed as he is bent over his work. His pencil moves almost involuntarily as he makes small random lines on his paper. [Robert] looks around the room as he says quietly to himself, "Stage, stage."

Becky puts her hand out in the air and sighs quietly. She is wait-
ing for assistance from a parent volunteer. Robert says to no one
in particular, "I'm going to cut out the giraffe."
　Becky says to the parent volunteer, "I'm through with this." The
aide responds, "It's okay." Becky asks, "How do I cut this out?" The
aide helps her, then leaves Becky to work on her own.
　Fred says to Robert, "That's not right! I got mine right." He
pushes his work in Robert's direction and says, "This is right. This
is right."
　Robert responds, looking at his own paper. "This ain't wrong."
He points at a problem as a parent volunteer passes by his table.
He says to the volunteer, "This is right, isn't it?" The aide examines
the paper and says, "You are right." Fred observes the interaction
and without saying anything to Robert begins to correct his work.

We were impressed with the program. Children in small groups
practiced what they had learned from the teacher, worked at tables in groups, and generally had fun. They got help when they
needed it and enjoyed a public display of accomplishment when
they finished their lessons. The teacher didn't have to intercede
even when the lights went out during the class.

The electricity goes out in the room. The students look up and
some question what's going on. However, there's not much com-
motion and enough light comes in through the windows to allow
students at most work situations to see what they're doing. Robert
says to his table (perhaps though he has a larger audience in
mind), "Don't worry, everything is under control." The lights go up
and then off again. Now the children stop working but they are being rather quiet. The teacher continues to work with a small
group. The lights go on again.
　Fred says to Robert, "It says for me to cut this out and I'm going
to cut out now." He takes a pair of blunt scissors and begins to cut
out an animal figure.

Lights are off again and Robert says repeatedly, "Relax, I've got everything under control. Everything's under control." As he works, he begins to cut out a paper figure on his worksheet. He turns to Becky and says, "You know what I've got? I've got some good news." Becky doesn't respond. Robert begins to whisper quietly to himself.

Fred is now working on another worksheet dealing with the *st* blend. He draws a house in the middle of the worksheet per instructions. When he's finished, he works on the questions at the bottom of the page. As he does so, he chants some blend sounds quietly to himself, "da, da, da, dot, da, dot."

Next to Robert, Fred whispers another set of words as he works on his assignment: "wet, net, vest, wet, man, met."

Becky says to her workmates, "This is all my work, now all I have to do is color." She seems proud. Fred looks up but does not respond. The lights are still off and Robert says, "I like the dark." Fred says, "You like working in the dark." Robert whispers, "Be quiet." Then he says, "It's fun resting in the dark," and he smiles. He begins to color. "I'm all done with my work. You need to color some of your stuff." He looks at Becky's work.

Fred says in a low voice, "Boom, brown, boom, brown."

Time is just about out and the teacher tells the class, "Begin finding a stopping place."

Fred: "Stopping place." Then he says to Becky, "You should be stopping. It's stopping time. The bell will ring in a second."

Teachers adjusted the program to fit their teaching styles and preferences. Thus the program was not identical in any two rooms. (It was voluntary, so some teachers didn't employ it at all. Those who did use the program seemed to have modified it to suit themselves.) Some teachers recruited parent volunteers and had one to three parents in the room almost every day. Other teachers didn't use parents at all. Some classes had eight centers, others had six. Some teachers individualized the work at most centers, others had all students progress through nearly identical material, at different rates.

In some classes students got immediate feedback on the work they completed. Volunteers would check the work as soon as it was completed, point out mistakes (often giving children a chance to correct them), praise work that was done correctly, and record the students' progress. In still other classes, teachers corrected the work at night.

All the teachers who employed the program liked it, though different teachers liked it for different reasons. All said that they had more time to concentrate on small-group instruction, and students had more time for productive practice. Some said they were more knowledgeable about how their students were doing than they had been in traditional classroom arrangements. Others said the program kept them organized and their students on task. Others emphasize the importance of parent involvement and how children benefited from immediate feedback. Some complained that they had to work too hard planning and organizing center material, but others said the program gave them back their evenings and weekends.

No doubt, it was a wise administrative decision not to force faculty to participate in the program or to insist that teachers carry out the program uniformly. Teachers who were not in the program told us they were not threatened by its existence and that they understood that there were no overt or subtle penalties for not participating. Teachers who joined up did not feel trapped or confined by the program. All reported that they felt they could modify the program to fit their teaching styles, and all said that their teaching had improved because of the program.

Improving teaching is a tricky business, but many decision makers today are impressed by programs that employ technology. It is as if they believe that systems that tightly regulate teacher behavior will force all teachers to teach well. By technology I mean nothing more than the application of scientific findings to practical programs. The program we have described here is an impressive piece of technology. It gives teachers a system of classroom organization and student practice that appears to have impressive results.

However, a word of caution is in order. I fear that my short description of the program does not do justice to what is probably its most important ingredient: the teacher. The program did not make these teachers good teachers; the teachers made this program a good program. In other words, the program is far from teacher-proof. It may help competent teachers become more effective, but it will not make incompetent teachers competent. The science of education provides no alchemy by which we can turn lead into gold. I'm going beyond the data here, but not far beyond. The teachers we observed use the program not as an organizational system but as a tool to monitor children's progress and to help students practice success. The teachers were all reflective practitioners. They monitored the program and modified it when it failed to work. Had they not been careful, had they not felt free to modify the program when necessary, I doubt the project would have been successful. The quality of the practice material could have been become bland and uniform, the movement from center to center might have become oppressively routine, aides might not have been adequately trained and organized, and teachers and students might have felt trapped rather than liberated by the program.

I do not say this to discourage anyone from adopting this program. Quite the contrary. I only emphasize the need to appreciate not only the intricacies of the system but also the capabilities of the teachers who designed and modified it. There is as much to be learned from their style and philosophy of invention as there is from the system they invented. They provide us with a message and a meta-message. The message is the system itself; the meta-

message is that teaching is a problem-seeing and problem-solving process. That process is not ended when we adopt a practice system or teaching method.

I want to end where I started. The system described here is not a recipe to be followed obediently by novice or compliant teachers. It will not replace professional intelligence. It is a tool that can aid our judgment and in that way help us improve our teaching. I am impressed by the system and by the intelligence of those who constructed (and reconstructed) it.

9

MANIPULATIVE MATERIALS IN THE TUTORING PROCESS

I(Carolyn Lawrence) retired from education ten years ago. Within my first year of retirement, I knew I needed and wanted to teach again. I started tutoring in my home. My preference for tutoring is children between the ages of about 6 and 10, but any child who is having trouble in reading or math I want to help.

My first tutoring student was Willie. At the time, Willie was 12 years old and was referred to me by a friend who said, "Willie has so much going for him personality-wise but can't read at all. He is very up-front about his inability to read and wants help." When I met him, he said, "I don't think I will ever be able to read. I really want to go to college and be in drama classes but I don't think I ever will because I can't read. I've always had trouble."

As a former teacher and principal, I have worked with many children individually and love to help them fill in the parts of the reading process they have missed in regular classroom instruction.

I have also demonstrated tutoring for my teachers. By the time I retired, I had accumulated many materials. Most of the materials I use in tutoring are listed in chapter 7. I also get surplus reading materials free from the school district warehouse. I love to use the old teacher's editions from a reading series. I especially appreciate all the examples they give for comprehension, decoding, and phonetic analysis.

I picked Willie up that first day, and we were comrades within the first hour, intent on overcoming his problems in reading. Even though only 12 years old, he was already streetwise, able to communicate very well, and had earned his own money for a few years. He mostly had to take care of himself because of a very poor home situation. He was tall for his age, uninhibited, as I am, and we had uninterrupted time to talk.

I said to him, "Willie, learning to read is just a matter of learning a few tricks, and I am going to teach you some of them. We'll start off with work that is too easy for you and then gets a little harder as we go along. This is going to take some time, so let's not rush it. I think we can have you reading pretty well within a year but you have to listen and work with me."

As I started working with him, I quickly found that he never learned to break down words and sound them out. He obviously was one of those children who could not readily commit words to memory just by looking at them, hearing them spoken, and attempting to write them—the process used to teach him in his elementary school. I am convinced that some children—especially those who come to school from homes where reading is not a part of daily family life—get left behind in reading when teachers are using the whole-language approach without teaching phonics skills as well. I love the whole-language approach, especially when it incorporates the writing process, but some children need specific help in cracking the code of written language to be able to understand how to break down words. Using the phonetic approach gives children who have difficulty some tricks, as I call them, to help them decipher words.

Willie was one of those children. Even though eager to learn, his attitude was "I don't think I will ever be able to read; I think I am just probably dumb." Willie definitely was not dumb and, I expect, had an above-average intelligence. I explained to him that sometimes students just need more help than others in the early years and teachers have too many students. Sometimes students get left behind and, as they get older, the upper-grade teachers do not have the knowledge of teaching reading as in the primary grades.

This is a problem throughout our schools in this country. I worked in 15 different elementary schools, and I found that unless a child gets a good foundation in reading before fourth grade, there is very little chance for that child to master the reading process without the kind of special help I was giving Willie. Reading foundation skills are taught from kindergarten through about third grade. After third grade, the children encounter a curriculum that assumes they have already mastered the foundation skills of reading. Teachers in the fourth grade and higher are more subject-matter specialists than reading specialists, and they generally have little knowledge of how to teach the foundation level of reading. They also have little time for giving individual attention to students who cannot read well enough and need extra help. The teaching of reading is a very arduous process that requires a lot of knowledge on the part of the teacher and must, for some children, be the focus of much time in the classroom.

With the advent of standardized testing and the emphasis on accountability, teachers must push to cover material so that children taking their tests in the spring will have covered everything that is on the test. Stopping to take time to try to teach a child to read is almost an impossibility. About the best a teacher can do is try to get the child tutored or refer the child for special testing that would help get additional service. These were the circumstances of Willie's schooling.

When Willie and I began working, I used a screening device that is called the Slosson Oral Reading test. I could quickly see that Willie was on an early second-grade level in reading. Basically, with Willie, as with all children, when I find they cannot attack new words, I start with the same process:

1. Give them the Slosson Oral Reading test to find out their correct instructional level.
2. Test them on beginning, ending, and vowel sounds. I used a screening sheet I developed with the alphabet letters mixed up and the vowels separate. It is reproduced below. This is discussed more extensively in my book *Literacy for All Children:*[1]

> Child names the letters to you as you use a duplicate copy of the test to mark mistakes, without the child seeing you mark the paper.
>
> You say, "See how many of these capital letters you can name for me":
>
> Z B C X P A S Y I D U M O L F V U H J Q E I G R K W
>
> "See how many of these lowercase letters you can name for me":
>
> w b r z k c g z i x e p q a j s n y t v d f u l d o m
>
> "Have you ever heard of a letter called a vowel? Name the five vowels."
>
> "Can you say the *long* sound of the five vowel letters—a e i o u?"
>
> "Can you say the *short* sound of the five vowel letters—a e i o u?"
>
> (With the short vowel sounds I usually draw them a picture to go with the sound, such as an apple to go with the short sound of *a*.)
>
> "Can you sound out any of these play words? Pud hiz lop wez fis cume tobe sole mote."

3. Teach them that vowels have two sounds: one short sound and one long sound. (This is simplistic, but teaching short words at first that fit this pattern gives children a start at deciphering words.)

4. Test them on the rules for breaking down words with one or two vowels. (Another simplistic rule that a child can grab onto when learning to read: Words with one vowel, such as *cap* usually have a short sound. If you add an *e* to the word *cap* then the vowel sound changes to the long vowel sound and makes the word *cape*.)

5. Emphasize over and over until they get it: if a word has two vowels, the first vowel usually says its name and the second vowel is silent. If a word has one vowel in the middle of a short word, the vowel is usually short.

After doing the above five things with Willie, I then got out the motivational hands-on materials for him to use in practicing the skills. Using the Stepboards, Versa-Tiles, and GeoSafari, Willie was able to practice breaking down small words. I started him on a first-grade level that he was able to handle comfortably. I cannot emphasize how important it is to establish a trust relationship with the child in the beginning of your tutoring.

Establishing trust is especially hard if a child has already had a bad experience with reading. For this reason, finding the correct instructional level of the child is paramount. After you find the correct instructional level, you should start the child *below* that level to give him or her many successful reading experiences in the beginning. Sometimes this may be even as simple as naming the letters of the alphabet. This first bond building is so much easier when you have different manipulative materials that appear to be games. Willie and I went straight to Stepboards, where he could practice what he already knew successfully first with beginning sounds.

Even though reading is a very complicated process, just learning these few rules gives children confidence that they can read new words. Using these rules, plus rhyming words, word patterns, and all the tricks that are in a teacher's manual, little by little, with successes at each step, a child begins to gain confidence. This is the beginning of the road to learning to read independently.

Willie and I worked once a week on Saturdays for about two hours, for about 18 months. Little by little, he began to learn to read. The progress was very slow, and he had to have much encouragement, and we had to go over rules for sounding out words many, many times. But Willie learned to read well enough to graduate. The last time I talked with him he had his own apartment, was enrolled at the community college, and was working in the drama department.

After working with Willie, I volunteered for a year at a public elementary school. I asked the first-grade teacher with whom I worked to give me her students who were having the most trouble in reading. As I watched her teach the whole-language approach to the whole class as a group, I could tell why some children who needed extra help were lost. The teacher was required to cover a certain number of books in the first grade and had to push the children along as fast as she could. Some of the children could not keep up with the pace, and these children began to get discouraged.

I worked with two boys. Both needed a lot of repetition and help with the basic skills of learning to read. As far as I could tell, both children were above average in intelligence, but both had been labeled *developmentally challenged*, the newest term in this school district for being behind academically.

There is a pattern in some classrooms to assign those developmentally challenged children to read with volunteers or aides, while the teacher works with the large group. I cannot stress enough that the teacher needs to be the one to work with these children who have problems in learning to read; the aides can be trained to carry the easier job—the reading instruction of the children who are reading at grade level.

Many children, especially those from affluent families, pick up reading very quickly without too much trouble. But some children have homes where reading is not the norm. Some get no exposure to print before entering school and have no sense that reading is important. These children must be taught how to break down words individually, and they need plenty of practice—all with the aim of finding comfort and enjoyment in reading.

I worked with these two first-grade boys for the remainder of the year. We had good times working together, and they enjoyed being able to progress slowly through the reading materials. I used manipulatives I brought from home plus the teacher's edition and charts. Unfortunately, they never did catch up to where they should have been by the end of the first grade, but they did get good foundation skills and were able to go to second grade. One boy moved away from the school for second grade, but when I checked, the other boy was managing in the second grade.

My next tutoring experience was with a child named Austen. My husband had a request from a friend who was running a small private school. He asked if I would consider coming to the school and helping a couple of the second-grade children learn to read. I went to the school once or twice a week for about six months to work with Austen and John. The school building was small, and we didn't have much room. Austen, John, and I, many times, enjoyed reading in the back of my van with the seats folded down to make a flat surface. Austen continued on with me after the school year, John did not.

Austen was an extremely bright child who had a disability in reading that had not been diagnosed. I didn't know she had a disability at the time I started working with her. The exact nature of her disability did not become clear, but the same formula worked with her that works with nearly all children who are stuck and delayed in reading. Building on self-esteem is always the first priority and then going from there to check to see where the gaps are in the basic reading skills.

Austen was and is exceptionally bright, and we started working and become good friends. At the end of the school year, she came to the house, where I had the materials. At the house we could work and read comfortably. She especially liked to climb on the bed while I was propped on pillows (I have severe arthritis and back problems), and we both used the teacher's edition to work on new skills. She was especially intrigued with the way new materials were highlighted in red for the teacher.

Austen and I became very good friends, and she would often spend the night in our guestroom when she didn't have school the next day. We would do some schoolwork, she would help me fold clothes, and she loved especially to wait on me if I was feeling bad. The adventure in learning to read seemed to her just something on the side, incidental to our friendship, and we grew very close.

Because I didn't feel Austen was getting the best education she could get at the private school, I asked her mother to consider sending her to public school. Her mother was reluctant at first. I promised that I would go with her to speak with Austen's teachers after Austen had been in school for a while. With some reluctance, she decided to put Austen in public school. After a few weeks of school, I went with her mother to speak with her teachers. As a former teacher and school principal, I was surprised and dismayed at how unreceptive school personnel can be. I wanted to talk frankly and openly about Austen's levels and problems in reading, but her teachers were emphatic that she was just not trying hard enough and could do much better.

Finally, with the assistant principal intervening, we got a program worked out for Austen that would allow her some flexibility for her learning disabilities—until she could be tested by the school psychologist. I remember one concession was that Austen could type her spelling words five times each instead of writing them five times each. Austen had a hard time with writing.

Thinking back to when Austen came to me, I remember we both loved to swim and after tutoring we would go into our pool and swim and talk. Austen was with me once a week for almost three years, and she is currently functioning well in a gifted class at her level in fifth grade in public school. I am happy for her.

I worked with Austen as I have with all children: teaching how to unlock words—which is basically a first-grade skill—and gradually using other materials and teacher's editions to expand the learning and the scope of the teaching to include reading, language arts, and especially writing skills. Austen and I often went to the public library to pick up books for me to read to her at first, and then later, when she was ready to branch out to reading on her own, we picked up books we thought she would enjoy reading to me. Besides the library books that she took home, Austen did some homework for me between most tutoring sessions—using the Homework Helper skill books I gave her. These are self-checking, self-pacing booklets with stickers in them to paste on completed pages (see chapter 5).

When I had been working with Austen for about two years, I was telling my veterinarian's assistant one day about how much I enjoyed tutoring. She said she had a sister named Mariah, a third grader, who just hated to read. She asked if I thought that I could help her, and so Mariah joined Austen.

Mariah, like all my other students, needed to learn the tricks about reading. Lacking them, she fumbled with reading, making guesses and mistakes she had no idea how to correct. She hated the confusion and lack of control she felt, and so she hated reading. She is a very intelligent child and just needed to fill in some gaps in her foundation for reading. Mariah's mom works with another nurse who has triplets who were then in the second grade.

She asked if I would consider taking the triplets along with Mariah. So for about a year I had Mariah, Austen, and the triplets.

This past summer my husband and I bought two acres of fenced land with a double-wide mobile home on it to make into a small school for me. It came with all the conveniences of a small house, and it is now converted into a one-room tutoring school. I still do not charge for the tutoring, but each parent pays me $10 a day for food and school supplies for each afternoon that we meet. During the school year, we meet one afternoon a week for about four hours and two afternoons during the summer.

I still have the triplets and Mariah. The triplets were born at only two pounds each and Mariah's mom actually helped deliver them. They are not only small, but also very behind academically, socially, and physically. All this is very understandable when you realize they were not expected to live, having been born three months early. The triplets names are Ashley, Brittney, and Caitlin. They were very shy and withdrawn. I am still working on getting them to talk freely and be outgoing, and with their mother's help they have made tremendous progress.

Angela, their mother, is a wonderful single mom who has a teenage son along with the girls. She cares very much about how well the girls do in school and works with them every night. I have even had to caution Angela about pushing the girls too hard. But the triplets, just this summer, after about two years, are now beginning to be good, independent readers. All three are repeating third grade next year but are making wonderful progress. The girls have thrived with the tutoring and enjoy coming.

As they have gotten the basic foundation for reading, they are branching off to read books we pick out together—to read to me and to take home from the public library. The summer tutoring consists of working on skills for about three hours and one hour of swimming, back at our house. I feed them lunch when they come to the school, we go over the day, and they do mastery centers with the manipulative kits, just exactly as I used to do in the classroom.

I regularly have two adult volunteer helpers, Pearl and Cathy. This summer, I have had the added advantage of having two teenage volunteer helpers. I have two neighborhood children, Stephanie and Hope, who have known me since they were about five years old. They are in advanced placement classes in high school now and need to earn community service hours to be in their courses in the tenth grade. They are thrilled to come and help with school twice a week. Stephanie guides whoever is in the typing skills center. I found an old electric typewriter at a garage sale for $10 and a table to put it on for another $10. Then I went to a used bookstore and was lucky to find a typing book very similar to the one I used when I learned typing in high school. The children absolutely adore their typing center and are becoming very efficient in putting their fingers in the right places for learning to type just by touch.

Our other centers include painting—just for fun—on an easel; GeoSafari stations; reading to Pearl who is 80 years old and loves to be with the children; practicing their multiplication tables; learning cursive writing; and doing other independent work, including writing and practicing skills with the other self-corrective materials. All the children also have a session of reading instruction with me when they are not in centers.

Within the last six months, I also picked up my grandson, who needed social contact and some help with math. He is flourishing at the tutoring school and loves the other children. Mariah has brought her good friend Savannah who is very smart but needs some help with math, especially fractions, and wants to come to the school. I also have a friend's son who is dyslexic and goes to a private school in Vermont during the year. William comes and helps the children read, and I pay him $5 an hour. He is also learning more reading skills for himself and becoming more outgoing from being shy at first.

With the help I have at the school, I look around during the school day and watch with true pride and happiness as the children work busily on their tasks. The variety in the centers helps them stay very focused. They know exactly how each center works, what is expected of them, and they know they will be changing to a new center every 25 minutes. Much of the feedback they receive from their work is immediate and gives them encouragement to continue to investigate and do good work. They are given much praise. My helpers and I watch and share about each child's needs and progress. It is pure joy for me to watch it all humming.

NOTE

1. Lawrence, C. M. (2004). *Literacy for All Children: A Formula for Leaving No Child Behind*. Lanham, MD: Scarecrow Education.

EPILOGUE:
OBSERVATIONS
OF CENTERS
20 YEARS LATER

The mastery centers program is not easily implemented—especially compared with just using textbooks and worksheets. It takes time, planning, consistency, and energy, but once the initial work is done, the teacher's job—the conscientious teacher's—is no more arduous or time consuming than conventional instruction.

Teachers who adopt the mastery centers approach seem to commit to it for their entire careers. I recently met a teacher when I was visiting her classroom because the principal told me that she was using mastery centers. The teacher did not know I had developed the centers program and had introduced it at her school, Spruce Creek Elementary in Port Orange, Florida, 20 years before when I was the assistant principal for instruction. It is a large elementary school of about 1,000 students. During the time I was assistant principal, I spent part of the day for three to

four weeks with each teacher as we worked together to change
over to the centers program. With my helping one teacher at a
time, along with the other assistant principal duties, launching
mastery centers in all the classrooms took about three years. This
was also the school where we set up a manipulatives resource center managed by the media center specialist from which teachers
could check out resources for their classroom mastery centers.

Now, 20 years later, as we entered the kindergarten teacher's
classroom, I saw that it was set up with chairs and tables arranged
for centers, and on the wall was the centers rotation chart we've
included in this book (see example 6.2). After visiting the classroom for about an hour and seeing how the children were doing
independently, I complimented her on how well her class organization worked and how nice it was to see children working so happily. She stated, "I have always used centers during these two
hours. I have from the first year I started teaching. I can't imagine providing children any other way. I developed this program almost years ago." I was delighted she had claimed
the program as her own. It was gratifying to see that she discov-
ered the importance of getting on each child's correct instructional level for practice work for mastery of skills.

Just about every teacher I have known who uses the centers
feels that the centers program is something that helps them provide for individual student differences better than any other system. Most have told me that before they used this program, they
did not know each child's strengths and weaknesses nearly as
well. When visiting schools where the program has been included
in the day-to-day routine of the children, I am intrigued by the
adaptations the teachers have made to make the program fit their
individual teaching styles.

Another teacher at Spruce Creek, Judy Degler, who has been
there for 25 years, was thrilled to show me her classroom as her

children worked in their centers. One incident reminded me of one of the positive effects of centers. A group of four children (heterogeneously grouped) was working using the GeoSafari geography materials listed in chapter 7. I quietly watched the group as it used cooperative learning and investigation. As they were working, the four children came over to Judy to show her with pride their accomplishment of completion. Although the GeoSafari materials give them feedback, the children had gone beyond what was being taught and, through their investigation, collectively came up with a question for clarification. Seeing these children talking softly as they worked together comfortably and with keen interest made me realize how little opportunity most children have for this kind of seatwork. As with all the centers materials listed in this book, the kit these children worked with had materials that were inviting and that gave immediate feedback as to whether answers were right or wrong. There is no punishment or stigma attached to wrong answers, simply a direction to go back and find out what works. Many materials give hints or clarification if the children can't get the answer after two wrong answers.

At the centers in Judy's room was a fraction of the self-managing materials for centers that she had accumulated—and had nicely stored in cabinets—to use periodically in changing out the content of the centers. There are countless such materials teachers can use, as long as they are sure that the children have been trained in the use of them, that the children mark their record cards, and that the materials are on the correct instructional level of the children.

Judy's classroom was busily humming with the excitement of learning as the children went to their particular stations, with Judy pulling individual children to help with specific skills. Her centers program was the same as the program described in this book with the exception of the rotation chart. She devised another way for the children to move from center to center. We talked for about 25 minutes as I observed the children in her classroom. She emphasized her love for the program and especially the fact that the children worked so cooperatively, with comfortable peer tutoring being the norm instead of competition or just indifference. When I first coached Judy in setting up the mastery centers, she was teaching first grade. Now she was teaching fourth grade. She told me the centers program was just as applicable in fourth grade as it had been in first grade. She showed me the different materials, and, as we talked and observed the centers, she told me she couldn't imagine teaching any other way.

I cannot emphasize enough the difference between a classroom such as Judy's and classrooms I have recently observed where children are all given the same seatwork. In Judy's and other similar classrooms, the quality of the children's attentiveness and relaxed concentration is reflected in their faces. They are clearly motivated and happy. The children are more on task practicing skills to mastery, and the amount of wasted time is kept to a minimum. They check most of their work themselves and correct it as needed without having to ask the teacher.

The materials do not teach the children but instead allow the children to practice to mastery the skills taught by the teacher. Many of the children who are faltering in a particular skill are taught by their peers with the cooperative way the centers are set up. When they use the materials correctly as they were trained to do, virtually no one is practicing errors or using skills the wrong way, no child is being defeated while doing seatwork, no child is being bored, and disruptive discipline problems are almost nonexistent.

The materials are so fun for the children, that at one point, as a school principal, I had to write a letter to the students' parents to explain that the children were indeed doing schoolwork and not "playing," as many of the children had told their parents they were doing.

As Judy and I talked, I was so happy to hear her say that getting children on the correct instructional level and having them work to mastery on their particular skill levels were of primary importance to her. So many teachers do not provide for various levels in a classroom, even though most intend to. A teacher cannot give direct instruction to five or six different instructional levels, but given the right materials in mastery centers, children can practice skills on their correct instructional level and keep a record of their own progress—a record the teacher can use to adjust the materials to match the progress.

After I met with Judy, I went to see another teacher whom I had started working with centers when I was at the school. Kathy McCarver is and was the special education teacher of physically and mentally handicapped children. Visiting her classroom was another thrilling experience. She uses centers, and the children were busily using many of the same manipulative kits I saw in the other classrooms. Kathy showed me the GeoSafari Laptop and exclaimed, "I just need a couple more of these laptops. The children love them and do such great work with them."

Seeing her classroom and Judy's classroom gave me such a warm feeling. The children were so happy. I went to several other classrooms in the school and saw they were all using some version of the centers program. The principal, Bonnie Lane, told me that the whole school is still using the program. It is very satisfying to see that the program has endured and is as relevant to today's children as it was two decades ago.

ABOUT THE AUTHORS

Carolyn M. Lawrence was born in Atlanta, GA. She was an elementary school teacher, reading supervisor, curriculum resource teacher, assistant principal for instruction, and elementary principal for 32 years in public education. In 1989, she was chosen as one of five outstanding educators in the country for her work with poverty-stricken children by the National Parent Teacher Association.

She is the author of *Literacy for All Children: A Formula for Leaving No Child Behind* (Lanham, MD: ScarecrowEducation, 2004). She and her husband, Gordon, live in Gainesville, FL. Lawrence currently writes and does volunteer tutoring.

Gordon Lawrence is a writer and consultant and a long-time educator. He grew up in Michigan but has been in Florida for the last 35 years, 20 of which as a professor of instructional leadership at the University of Florida. His special interest is in the research on communication patterns and what makes classroom instruction effective. Author of numerous books and articles, he is now writing a book on motivation patterns.

Linda S. Samek was born on Long Island, NY, where she worked as a registered nurse at the State University of New York Stony Brook. She came to Florida in 1974 and continued nursing until she received her master's degree in education from Stetson University.

Samek began teaching in 1980 and has worked specifically as a teacher for troubled youth (ALPHA), third, fourth, and fifth grades, and is presently a math fusion laboratory teacher. Her career for the last 25 years has been devoted to making instruction practical and fun for children.

Samek gives workshops for teachers and supervisors in Florida and other states. She teaches in the less affluent schools by choice and is honored by her peers and supervisors in Florida. She is a member of the National Association of Teacher Education, Phi Delta Kappa, Volusia County Reading Association, Florida Teachers of Math, and Volusia County Teachers of Math.